Mi Fu on Ink-stones

Other titles by R. H. van Gulik, available from Orchid Press:

Crime and Punishment in Ancient China: *T'ang-Yin-Pi-Shih*

Hayagriva: Horse Cult in Asia

Scrapbook for Chinese Collectors: A Chinese Treatise on Scrolls and Forgers

The Lore of the Chinese Lute: An Essay in the Ideology of the Ch'in

R. H. van Gulik biography available from Orchid Press:

Dutch Mandarin: The Life and Work of R. H. van Gulik

Mi Fu on Ink-stones

TRANSLATED BY

R. H. van Gulik

WITH AN INTRODUCTION AND NOTES

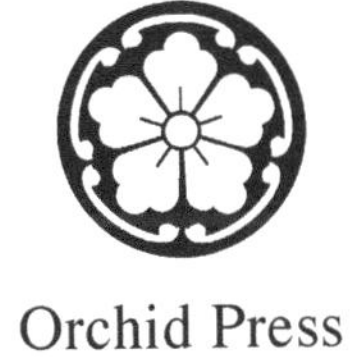

Orchid Press

MI FU ON INK-STONES
Translated with an introduction and notes by R. H. van Gulik

First published by Henri Vetch, Peking, 1938

Second imprint, 2006

ORCHID PRESS
P.O. Box 19
Yuttitham Post Office
Bangkok 10907, Thailand

www.orchidbooks.com

Front cover: Ink-stone in the form of a winnowing basket (*ji xing yan*); Duan type stone (see index: *Tuan-hsi*), Tang Dynasty; private collection, Hong Kong.

ISBN 978-974-524-155-8

CONTENTS

ILLUSTRATIONS

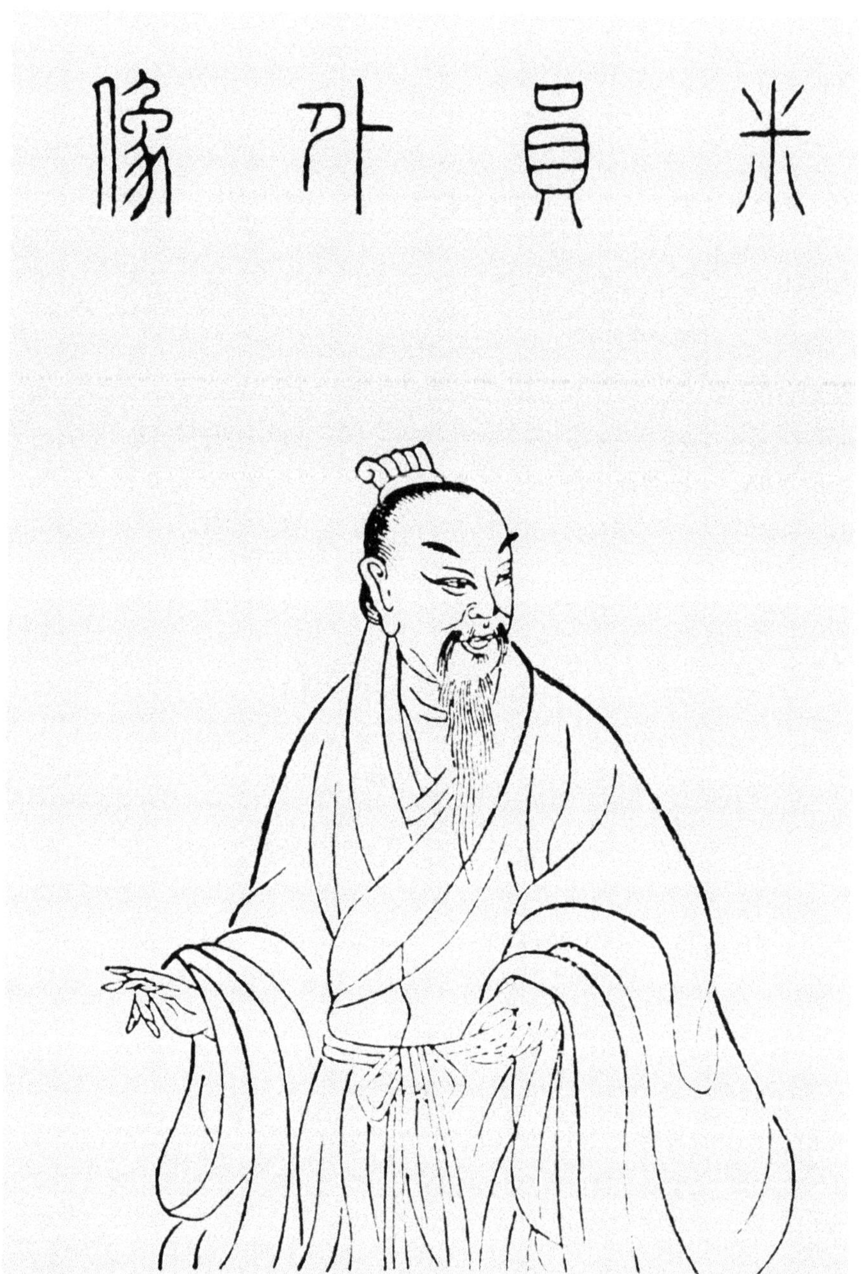

MI FU
From a picture in the *Wu-chün-ming hsien-t'u-chuan-tsan*,
(completed in 1888)

PREFACE

THIS monograph on Mi Fu and his treatise on ink-stones does not pretend to be anything more than a preliminary study of the subject. To my translation of his *Yen-shih*, "An Account of Ink-stones" (Chapter III), I have added a survey of his literary activities, a list of some secondary sources of information relating to him (Chapter I), and a few remarks on the Chinese inkslab, in general (Chapter II). Lastly, in Chapter IV, I have attempted to draw some general conclusions from these materials, and particularly from the *Yen-shih*.

The field of Chinese literature is so vast that a first attempt to collect data on any subject must needs remain incomplete. Mi Fu, however, occupies such a prominent place in the history of Chinese pictorial art, that I feel justified in venturing to publish the result of my investigations.

Mi Fu founded a school of painting by virtue of his exquisite landscapes. His typically heavy brushwork, however bold and vigorous, enhances the delicate dreaminess which his studies convey. Originals of his paintings seem, unfortunately, to be rare; but the same bold technique is characteristic of his handwriting, of which happily, original specimens still exist. In both painting and calligraphy he founded a school which was named after him. His son Mi Yu-jên 米友仁 (style: Yüan-hui 元暉, 1086-1165) continued the style of his father, and shares part of his fame.

In later times Mi Fu found many ardent admirers. The first seems to have been the Yüan painter Ni Tsan 倪瓚 (style: Yüan-chên 元鎮, 1301-1374). He followed Mi Fu's technique in painting, and even went so far as to copy Mi Fu in matters of personal fastidiousness (*chieh-p'i* 潔癖: cf. *Ch'ing-pi-ko-ch'üan-chi* 淸閟閣全集, ch. XII).

The Ming scholars Mao Chin (*v. infra*, page 3) and Fan Ming-t'ai (*infra*, page 4) devoted much time to collecting materials relating to Mi Fu, and published several volumes containing stories current about him and his works. Later, Chang Ch'ou (*infra*, page 3) considered Mi Fu as the paragon of old painters, and even chose, for his own literary name, Mi-an 米庵, i.e. "The scholar from the hermitage where Mi Fu is studied."

Finally the Ch'ing scholar Wêng Fang-kang (*infra*, page 11) extracted from his extensive collection of references to Mi Fu a detailed biography of the painter.

In Japan he also found many followers. One of the best known is Ichikawa Sangai (市川三亥, 1777-1854), a famous Yedo calligrapher, who, in Japan, is considered as the great advocate of *kansho* 漢書, the Chinese style of writing, as opposed to *washo* 和書 the Japanese style, which had become popular during the Tokugawa period. He published a small book on the technique of Mi Fu's calligraphy entitled *Beika-shoketsu* 米家書訣, printed in Kyōto in 1801. Ichikawa, too, adopted the literary name 米庵 Beian.

In this treatise I have cursorily discussed some of the materials that were collected by these people. I must apologize for the dryness of this enumeration: since, however, this study is but a first step, I have felt compelled to document all information rather extensively, in order to facilitate further research.

It goes without saying that the subject is far from being exhausted. I publish this essay in the hope that it may induce other workers in the same field to continue the study of this subject, correcting and amplifying the results of my researches.

I avail myself of this opportunity to express my feelings of gratitude to His Excellency Hsü Shih-ying, Ambassador of the Chinese Republic in Tōkyō, who kindly wrote the superscription to this essay, and who has been good enough always to encourage me in my Chinese studies.

In conclusion, I wish to thank Mr. Henri Vetch for many valuable suggestions.

DR. R. H. VAN GULIK

TŌKYŌ, DECEMBER 1, 1936.

寶賢良之美質
擅大雅之隆名

中華民國二十五年九月為
高羅佩先生著米海岳硯史考題

雙谿許世英

Note

In Chapter III the Chinese text of the *Yen-shih* has been printed horizontally, from left to right. The fact that since olden times the Chinese characters were normally written vertically, has, it is true, impressed itself to such an extent on the style and construction of the characters that they are more easy to read when printed in vertical columns. But in a case like the present one, where passages in Chinese are alternated with their English translation, it proves tiring continually to skip from the horizontal English to the vertical Chinese, which demands a new adjustment of the eye. Therefore, I had the Chinese text printed horizontally, and in my opinion this method is to be recommended in all such cases.

To give a general idea of the appearance of ink-stones, and in order to explain some terms which occur in the *Yen-shih*, I have added illustrations of some old stones. Not trusting my own judgment in the difficult question of appreciating and selecting ink-stones, I decided to use rubbings of ink-stones collected by Chi Yün 紀昀 (style: 曉嵐 Shao-lan, 1724-1805), the great scholar under whose direction the Imperial Catalogue *Ssû-k'u-ch'üan-shu-tsung-mu* was compiled. Rubbings of some representative stones of his famous collection, with his appreciations engraved on them, were published by his grandson under the title *Yüeh-wei-ts'ao-t'ang-yen-pu* 閱微草堂硯譜. The scholar and statesman Hsü Shih-ch'ang 徐世昌 added a preface dated 1916.

I inserted a number of diagrams of some usual shapes of ink-stones. (*see* pages 16, 17, and also the index, *s.v. Types*).

LIST OF ABBREVIATIONS

S. K.	*Ssû-k'u-ch'üan-shu-tsung-mu* 四庫全書總目, edition of 1930, 10 vols., published in Shanghai by the Ta-tung-shu-chü 大東書局.
C. F. C. W.	*Ch'ün-fang-ch'ing-wan* 羣芳清玩, Ming edition, see page 15.
F. Y. S.	Fan Ming-t'ai's compilation: *Mi-hsiang-yang-chih-lin* 米襄陽志林, see page 4.
H. C. T. Y.	*Hsüeh-chin-t'ao-yüan* 學津討原, Compilers' preface dated 1805; see page 15.
M. S. T. S.	*Mei-shu-ts'ung-shu* 美術叢書, second edition, 1928; see page 15.
S. F.	*Shuo-fu* 說郛, revised edition, preface dated 1646; see page 15.

CHAPTER I

INTRODUCTION

AMONG the many illustrious artists of the Sung period Mi Fu 米芾 (1051-1107), the famous painter, is one of the most attractive, because of his many-sided and very interesting personality.

Not only does he rank high among Chinese landscapists and calligraphers, but he is also esteemed as a poet and essayist, while tradition calls him one of the most discerning of collectors and connoisseurs.

Remarks on him and his works may be found in most occidental handbooks on Chinese painting,[1] but the data given therein seem to be too fragmentary to convey to the reader a sufficiently clear idea of Mi Fu's[2] personality. Like, unfortunately, most Chinese painters, he remains for the western student merely a name, with which are connected a few dates, some famous paintings and a certain style—the personal note being supplied by anecdotes of doubtful authenticity. It seems that enough books have already been written on the subject of Chinese painting, in general, and the time has now come to consider the many outstanding Chinese artists, individually.[3] In Chinese literature, rich materials of great documentary value are available. Contemporary or later critics and literati wrote long dissertations about painters, collecting and publishing rubbings of their handwriting and of their drawings, which were reproduced on stone or other materials, and they added copious æsthetic and historical notes. Most of this information, scattered through widely different sources, is collected in the *nien-piao* 年表 (also called *nien-pu* 年譜) or " biographical accounts." These *nien-piao* are the product of patient and careful research in the

---

[1] Most detailed is O. Sirén: *A History of early Chinese Painting*, London 1933, part II; further, of the same author, *The Chinese on the Art of Painting*, Peiping 1936, pp. 66-69 *et passim*.

[2] The transcription *Fu* I have discussed below: *v.* page 12.

[3] The *Ostasiatische Zeitschrift* has published some well-documented illustrated articles on Chinese painters; I mention especially *T'ang Yin*, by Werner Speiser, 1935, Nos 1-2 and 3-4.

vast field of Chinese literature. They are chronologically arranged: under each year are recorded the whereabouts of the person at that time, the paintings he produced, the essays or poems he wrote, the colophons (*pa* 跋) or superscriptions (*t'i* 題) he added to paintings or scrolls done by other artists, etc. Numerous *nien-piao* have been compiled, minutely describing the life and works of the most famous of the old Chinese artists.

Frequently the painters themselves were successful authors, and their works are preserved, sometimes in their own handwriting.

Finally, there are the old Chinese histories of painting, abounding in interesting details, which, as yet, no one has begun to translate.

To verify and interpret all of these materials presents a laborious task. But the result will be that we shall see an old Chinese painter as a historical character, as a human being, and not merely as "the man who painted the so-and-so scroll." Moreover, these data constitute the necessary foundation upon which the judging of the authenticity of an old painting must be based. Æsthetic criteria, I wish to point out clearly in this connection, are in this respect insufficient. On the other hand, the æsthetic appreciation of an old masterpiece will be deepened when one knows the personality of the painter. And I am firmly convinced that when the work of critical historical research has been completed we shall see many an old painting in quite another light.

For Mi Fu the material is especially rich and varied. Unfortunately his complete literary works were lost at an early date, according to the well-known Sung scholar Yo K'o 岳珂 (style: Su-chih 肅之; *hao*: Chüan-wêng 倦翁, 1173-1240) in his introduction (dated 1232) to the *Pao-chin-ying-kuang-chi* 寶晋英光集. The latter represents the remnants of an older collection, which was called *Shan-lin-chi* 山林集, and consisted of a hundred chapters; the present collection contains only eight chapters, with one supplement.[1] Inspite of its being imperfect this *Pao-chin-ying-kuang-chi* gives a fairly good idea of Mi Fu's literary achievements: it contains lyrical descriptions (*fu* 賦), poems (*shih* 詩), prefaces (*hsü* 序), descriptive pieces (*chi* 記), eulogies (*tsan* 贊), inscriptions on memorial stones (*pei* 碑), superscriptions and colophons (*t'i-pa* 題

[1] Cf. the discussion of this question in *S.K.*, ch. 154, page 6, and also the remarks of Lu Hsin-yüan 陸心源 (*v. infra* p. 18), in: *Pi-sung-lou-ts'ang-shu-chih* 皕宋樓藏書志, ch. 27.

跋), miscellaneous pieces (*tsa-cho* 雜著), and various essays (*wên* 文). It has been preserved in a *ts'ung-shu* of the Hsien-fêng 咸豐 period (1851-1861), entitled *Shê-wen-tzû-chiu* 涉聞梓舊 [in exactly the same form in the modern *ts'ung-shu: Hu-pei-hsien-chêng-i-shu* 湖北先正遺書], and in the collection of Mi Fu's works published by Fan Ming-t'ai (*v. infra*).

Many of Mi Fu's poems, moreover, are preserved in separate collections: there are the *Mi-hsiang-yang-shih-chi* 米襄陽詩集, to be found in the Ming collection *Sung-yüan-ming-chia-shih-chi* 宋元名家詩集; the *Hsiang-yang-shih-ch'ao* 襄陽詩鈔 (one chapter), in the *Sung-shih-ch'ao* 宋詩鈔, and, as an addition to this, the *Hsiang-yang-shih-pu-ch'ao* 襄陽詩補鈔, in the *Sung-shih-ch'ao-pu* 宋詩鈔補. A further supplement is contained in the Ch'ing *ts'ung-shu: Chiang-ts'un-ts'ung-shu* 彊村叢書, compiled by Chu Tsu-mou 朱祖謀 (1857-1921), and is called *Pao-chin-ch'ang-tuan-chü* 寶晉長短句.

Descriptions of and comments on his paintings may be found in many later works on the history of Chinese painting.[1] Most thorough seems to be what Chang Ch'ou 張丑 (original name: Ch'ien-tê 謙德; style: Shu-i 叔益) has given in his *Ch'ing-ho-shu-hua-fang* 清河書畫舫 (preface dated 1616), where all sources are carefully mentioned. Moreover the *Pao-chang-tai-fang-lu* (*v. infra* page 9) is reprinted there.

Further, there are certain collections of anecdotes about Mi Fu, sometimes combined with current stories about the other famous Sung painter Su Tung-p'o. Widely known is the Ming collection *Su-mi-chih-lin* 蘇米志林 compiled by Mao Chin 毛晉 (original name Feng-pao 鳳苞; style: Tzû-chin 子晋, 1599-1659), and discussed *S.K.*, ch. 60, page 6. My copy consists of six small books, four treating of Su Tung-p'o, and the other two containing materials relating to Mi Fu.[2] Mao Chin observes in a colophon that for ten years he had tried to obtain a (complete) copy of the *Pao-chin-chai-chi* 寶晉齋集 (probably the same

[1] A good survey of Mi Fu's paintings as mentioned in Chinese sources is to be found in the *Li-tai-cho-lu-hua-mu* 歷代著錄畫目, by J. C. Ferguson (Peiping 1933), where under Mi Fu 164 items are given.

[2] It is of bibliographical interest to note that of editions the wood-block carving of which was supervised by Mao Chin, this is one of the few which have in the margin the characters Lü-chün-t'ing 綠君亭, instead of the usual Chi-ku-ko 汲古閣. Cf. also *Shu-lin-ch'ing-hua* 書林清話, ch. 7, under: 明毛晉汲古閣刻書之六.

collection as the *Shan-lin-chi* 山林集 mentioned above), but without success. He therefore apologizes for the fact that what he offers is merely a compilation of desultory remarks, culled from secondary sources, superscriptions and colophons on scrolls, anecdotes, etc.

Approximately the same material is found in two works of Kuo Hua 郭化: the *Su-mi-t'an-shih* 蘇米譚史, and the *Su-mi-t'an-shih-kuang* 蘇米譚史廣, the introduction to the first of which is dated 1611 (cf. *S.K.*, ch. 60, page 5). These two books I have not seen myself.

Further *S.K.* mentions three books concerning Mi Fu compiled by Fan Ming-t'ai 范明泰 (style: Ch'ang-k'ang 長康; received *chü-jên* 舉人 in 1600): they are the *Mi-hsiang-yang-wai-chi* 米襄陽外集, *Mi-fu-chih-lin* 米芾志林 (*S.K.*, ch. 60, page 5), and *Hsiang-yang-i-chi* 襄陽遺集 (*S.K.*, ch. 174, page 9). I have not seen these three books in separate editions, but I possess a Ming copy of a work entitled *Mi-hsiang-yang-chih-lin* 米襄陽志林, the blocks of which were cut under the supervision of Fan himself, and in the first part of which the three books mentioned above are united in 17 chapters, and their contents to a certain extent rearranged; the second part, *Huang-yü-chang-chih-lin* 黄豫章志林 contains anecdotes about the literatus and calligrapher Huang T'ing-chien 黄庭堅 (1045-1105). As one of his sources for the part on Mi Fu, Fan Ming-t'ai mentions in his Introduction (dated 甲辰, probably 1604) a book entitled *Nan-kung-i-shih* 南宮遺事 by Lu Yu-jên 陸友仁 (*circa* 1600), which I have not yet been able to trace. In my copy of the *Mi-hsiang-yang-chih-lin* the *Hai-yo-ming-yen*, the *Pao-chang-tai-fang-lu*, and the *Yen-shih* are also incorporated. The well-known literatus Ch'ên Chi-ju 陳繼儒 (style: Chung-shun 仲醇, 1558-1639) added an introduction.

Not having seen the three books mentioned in *S.K.*, I am unable to decide in what relation these works by Fan Ming-t'ai stand to his *Mi-hsiang-yang-chih-lin*. Judging by his introduction to the latter work, however, I am inclined to believe that the three books were the results of Fan's previous researches, which he wrote a résumé of and completed in his *Mi-hsiang-yang-chih-lin*.

The anecdotes about Mi Fu widely quoted in Chinese and occidental handbooks on painting are mainly borrowed from collections like those enumerated here. But as such books do not mention their sources, they should be used with great discretion. It goes without saying that until these collections are critically examined, one is hardly justified in using quotations from them in order to give an idea of Mi Fu's personality.

Finally numerous manuscripts of Mi Fu have been preserved in his own handwriting or in copies. The study of these documents, together with the investigation of the various seals which Mi Fu used to print on them, is very important for the art-historian : for, by comparing Mi Fu's ordinary writing in letters to his friends, etc., with the signatures on his paintings, one may obtain safe criteria for judging the authenticity of the latter. Of the manuscripts, many specimens are now published in photographic reproductions of the originals. I mention, e.g., the beautiful photographic edition of the *Mi-nan-kung-t'iao-hsi-shih* 米南宮苕溪詩, published by the Yen-kuang-shih 延光室 in Peking. Several photographic editions of authentic manuscripts of Mi Fu, and of good rubbings of his work, have been published by the Wên-ming-shu-chü 文明書局 of Shanghai. The Japanese calligraphic collection *Shodō-zenshu* 書道全集 (Heibonsha 平凡社, 1926) gives in part XVIII some very well selected specimens, and in particular some good photographs of Mi Fu's seal.

Since ancient times, however, the most popular way of reproducing famous scrolls has been to publish them as rubbings (*t'a-pên* 搨, 拓本). As material for research, rubbings are, of course, far less reliable than manuscripts. When a scholar had collected a number of manuscripts of famous calligraphers, he would give them to a special artisan, who carved the text in wood. First a sheet of thin paper was laid over the original, and then the contours of each stroke were carefully traced [this process is called *shuang-kou* 雙鉤]. After this tracing, the letters were carved in a wooden block, *tsao-mu* 棗木 or date-wood being mostly used. Copies were obtained by putting a sheet of moistened paper over the wood, and rubbing this with a cake of ink. When a scroll had become so grimy with age as to be illegible, it was hung against the window of a darkened room, and a piece of thin paper suspended over it: the tracing was done by a man sitting inside the room—a method known as *hsiang-t'a* 嚮搨. Rubbings were also taken from rock-inscriptions and from stone-tablets. The quality of a rubbing depends entirely upon the skill of the man who did the carving: every splash, every small irregularity that gives a piece of calligraphy its special character, should be reproduced with the utmost fidelity. Often, however, the carver changed or completed certain strokes according to his own fancy and often also impressions of seals were left out. Afterwards other people, on the basis of the first rubbing, carved the text for a second time, and this went on until the rubbings obtained differed widely from the original manuscript.

Mi Fu himself warns against the use of rubbings. He says: "One should not study rubbings. Even if one has one's own writing carved in stone, it is not like the original. Therefore one should study the original manuscripts: only then can one capture their spirit. For instance, Yen Chên-ch'ing 顏眞卿 (style: Ch'ing-ch'ên 淸臣; 709-784;

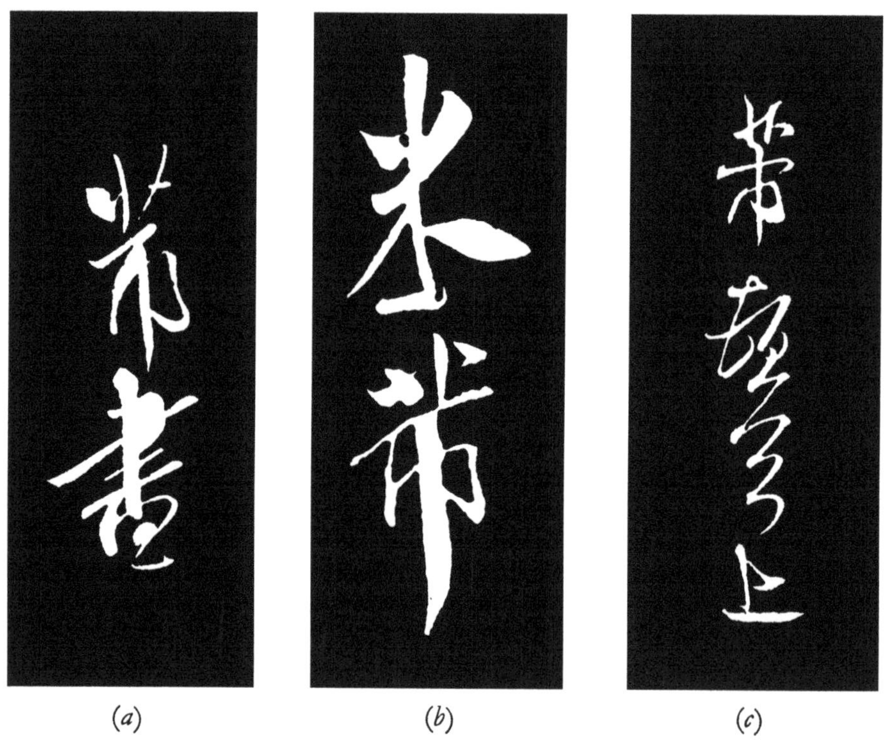

(*a*) (*b*) (*c*)

I.—Mi Fu's Signature

(*a*) *Fu shu* 芾書, "Mi Fu wrote"; (*b*) Mi Fu;
(*c*) *Fu tun shou shang* 芾頓首上, "Mi Fu offers, bowing down."

one of the masters of Chinese calligraphy) used to make his serving boys carve his writings : because they knew the mind of their master, they corrected the strokes that had not succeeded well, to such a degree

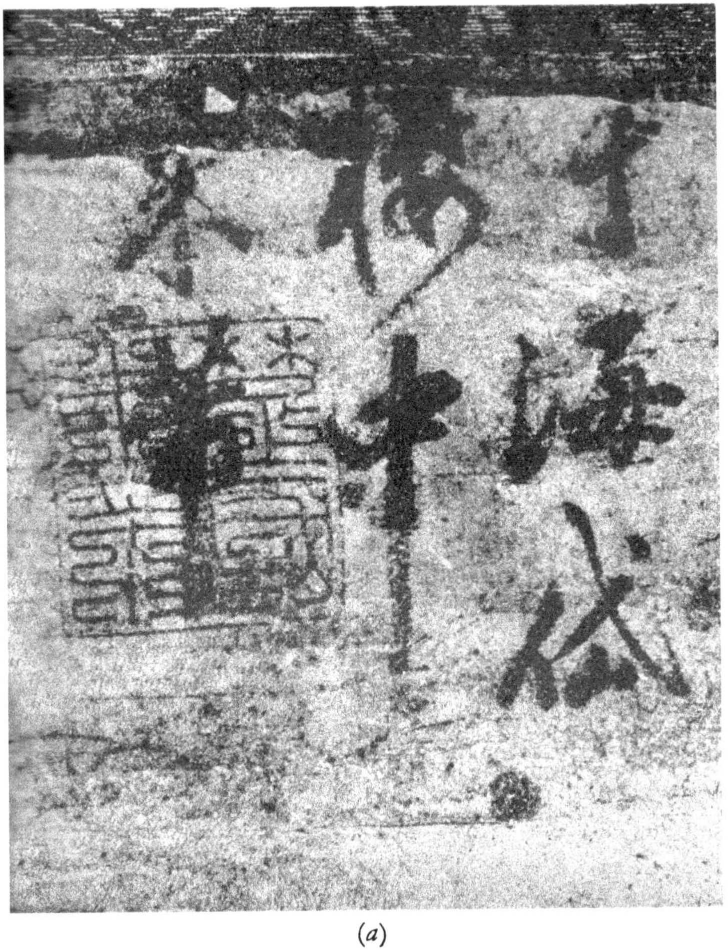

(*a*)

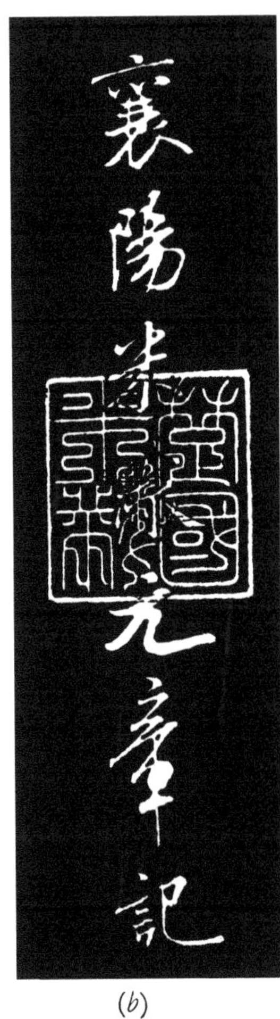

(*b*)

II.—Mi Fu's Signature and Seal.

(*a*) According to an original manuscript (collection of Mr. Fusetsu Nakamura, Tokyo), Mi Fu 米芾, whilst the seal reads Ch'u-kuo Mi Fu 楚國米芾; this is also the reading of the seal on the cover of this book, taken from a writing by Mi Fu, preserved in the National Museum at Mukden. (*b*) According to a San-hsi-t'ang 三希堂 rubbing, *Hsiang yang Mi Fu Yüan-chang chi* 襄陽米黻元章記, whilst the seal reads : Ch'u-kuo Mi Fu 楚國米黻

that much of the spirit of the original was lost" (*Hai-yo-ming-yen*, 8th heading: 石刻不可學。但自書使人刻之, 已非已書也。故必須眞跡觀之, 乃得趣。如顏眞卿每使家僮刻字, 故會主人意, 修改披撆致大失眞).

As Mi Fu's style of writing was much admired, hundreds of different rubbings of the same text exist in book form: compared with the original manuscript there are but few that give a tolerable reproduction. Since, however, his manuscripts are rare, and only a few have been published in photographic reproductions, we must depend largely upon rubbings for the study of his writing and seals. I shall therefore mention here some of the best known collections of rubbings made from Mi Fu's writings. The most reliable collection is to be found in the *Hsi-hung-t'ang-fa-shu* 戲鴻堂法書, being the collection of the Ming artist Tung Ch'i-ch'ang 董其昌 [style: Hsüan-t'sai 玄宰; 1555-1636; cf. V. Contag, *Tung Ch'i-ch'ang's Hua-ch'an-shih-sui-pi und das Hua-shuo des Mo Shih-lung, Ostasiatische Zeitschrift*, 1922]; many rubbings taken directly from inscriptions after Mi Fu's writing and provided with his correct seals, are to be found in chap. 14. Again, reliance may be placed in the old Imperial collection of rubbings of the San-hsi-t'ang 三希堂. Specimens of Mi Fu's writing are published under the name of *San-hsi-t'ang-mi-nan-kung-fa-shu* 三希堂米南宮法書; but one should be careful to choose good editions. Rather extensive, but not so reliable is the *Pai-yün-chü-mi-t'ieh* 白雲居米帖, which represents a collection of rubbings belonging to the scholar Yao Shih-fêng 姚式峰, and collected in 1728.

In Chinese literature Mi Fu the art-critic is as famous as Mi Fu the artist and scholar. This aspect of Mi Fu's intellectual activity, by which his significance is raised above that of an individual painter to that of a historian of the whole of Chinese painting before his time, may be studied in his own critical compositions.

Mi Fu devoted two separate critical works to painting and calligraphy, the two subjects which lay nearest to his heart: the *Hua-shih* 畫史 "An Account of Painting," and the *Shu-shih* 書史 "An Account of Calligraphy." These books contain a wealth of valuable information, though in fragmentary form, on various artists, and their works and methods, and especially give much technical details.

Some passages from these books, which are widely quoted in Chinese literature, have also found their way into occidental treatises on Chinese painting; but as I pointed out above, such fragments are worthless when not considered in their context. The *Hua-shih* in particular should be translated in its entirety. The texts of these two books are so well known that I need not enumerate here the various editions; I would, however, draw attention to the carefully punctuated edition of the *Hua-shih* in the Japanese collection *Keisetsuken-ronga-sōsho* 螢雪軒論畫叢書, published by Kondō Gansui 近藤元粹 in 1911.

Further, Mi Fu added many superscriptions and colophons to various famous paintings and scrolls. Many of these are to be found in the *Pao-chin-ying-kuang-chi* mentioned above. A special collection is constituted by the *Hai-yo-t'i-pa* 海岳題跋, "Superscriptions and Colophons by Mi Fu," which is included in the *Chin-tai-pi-shu* 津逮秘書, a *ts'ung-shu* of the Ming period. The compiler was Mao Chin 毛晉 (*v. supra*), who, in his introduction to this book, praises the knowledge and the sharp eye of Mi Fu, saying that once Mi Fu criticized in a colophon a scroll, any doubt as to its authenticity was removed. This text is reprinted in the same form in the collection *Hu-pei-hsien-chêng-i-shu* (*v. supra*). In 1921 Wu I 吳頤 published a new edition, revised on the basis of a rare original copy, the wood blocks of which were cut and supervised by Mao Chin.

Among Mi Fu's critical writings his *Pao-chang-tai-fang-lu* 寶章待訪錄 must also be mentioned. This is a collection of critical descriptions of a great number of scrolls, and was completed in 1086. It is to be found in the *ts'ung-shu* entitled *Pai-ch'uan-hsüeh-hai* 百川學海 (preface dated 1273), and in the same form in the *Hu-pei-hsien-chêng-i-shu*, as well as in the *Mei-shu-ts'ung-shu*, v. page 10, and in Fan Ming-t'ai's compilation (*v. supra*, p. 4). Whereas in his *Shu-shih* and *Hua-shih* Mi Fu discussed together not only scrolls which he had actually investigated but also scrolls which he had not seen, in the *Pao-chang-tai-fang-lu* he treats the two categories separately, calling the first *mu-tu* 目覩: "What I have seen with my own eyes," and the second *ti-wên* 的聞: "What I have learned from reliable sources."

In the small treatise *Hai-yo-ming-yen* 海岳名言, "Famous sayings of Mi Fu," a number of his pronouncements on calligraphy and calligraphers are collected. This book is found in the same three *ts'ung-shu* as the *Pao-chang-tai-fang-lu*, mentioned above, and in Fan Ming-t'ai's compilation.

Finally, Mi Fu was highly interested in the technique of painting and calligraphy. The *Hua-shih* and *Shu-shih* abound in observations on the various kinds of silk to be used for painting, on ink, on brushes, etc. Furthermore, there is a small collection of separate remarks of his on several sorts of paper—the *P'ing-chih-t'ieh* 評紙帖—preserved in his own handwriting: *v. Pao-chin-ying-kuang-chi*, supplement. This text is also contained in the *Mei-shu-ts'ung-shu* 美術叢書.

He also wrote a small treatise specially devoted to the inkslab. This book, which is called *Yen-shih* 硯史, "An Account of Ink-stones," constitutes, notwithstanding its briefness, a worthy pendant to his *Hua-shih* and his *Shu-shih*.

The *Yen-shih* I have attempted to translate below. The reason why I chose this small book, which at first sight seems to be the least interesting, is that this essay may well furnish us with the most important material about Mi Fu's critical methods. For the data given therein may be verified. Whereas his *Hua-shih*, for example, discusses paintings which for the most part have been lost, even in copies, old ink-stones, on the other hand, are still preserved in large numbers. For many centuries, ink-stones have been cherished by art-collectors; and in museums and private collections countless old stones may be seen in excellent condition. As there are among them many specimens that date from the T'ang and Sung periods, we can actually see and study the same material as lay before Mi Fu. By comparing his observations on the objects with the objects themselves, and by judging the methods he used in treating this material, we shall be able to form an opinion as to the value of his critical studies in other fields.

Before going further, however, with this subject, I think it might not be without interest to try first to settle here a question regarding Mi Fu in general, viz. the right pronunciation of his name.

I have spoken above of the *nien-piao* or biographical sketches, where detailed descriptions are given of the lives of prominent people, chronologically arranged. The *nien-piao* of Mi Fu was compiled by a capable scholar, the Ch'ing official and literatus Wêng Fang-kang[1] 翁方綱 (style: Chêng-san 正三; *hao*: T'an-ch'i 覃谿; 1733-1818): the title of the book is *Mi-hai-yo-nien-pu*[2] 米海岳年譜, and it is published in the *Yüeh-ya-t'ang-ts'ung-shu* 粵雅堂叢書 [there is a colophon dated 1855 by the editor of the *ts'ung-shu*]. In his quality of provincial examiner,—first as *hsiang-shih* 鄉試, examiner at the triennial examinations in the provincial capital, and later as *hsüeh-chêng* 學政, director of the schools of a province, and examiner for the degree of *hsiu-ts'ai* 秀才,—Wêng Fang-kang travelled extensively in different parts of China, and therefore had the opportunity of collecting various literary and historical data on the spot. This *nien-piao*, which he compiled in his later years, is a good specimen of literary research, being a collection of reliable information supported by quotations from authoritative sources.

---

[1] Cf. *Kuo-ch'ao-hsien-chêng-shih-lüeh* 國朝先正事略, ch. 41.

[2] Hai-yo was one of the many *hao* 號 or literary names of Mi Fu, in full: Hai-yo-wai-shih 海岳外史, "The petty official of Hai-yo," Hai-yo referring to the name of a library of his, the Hai-yo-an 海岳庵. Mi Fu also designated himself by literary names derived from other names of his study, e.g. Shan-lin-t'ang, 山林堂, "The Hall of the Mountain Forest"; Ching-ming-chai 淨名齋, "The Studio of the Pure Name" [this probably refers to the Bodhisattva *Vimalakirti*; for Mi Fu was interested in Buddhism]; Pao-chin-t'ang 寶晉堂, "The Hall where Chin calligraphy is treasured" [referring to the fact that Mi Fu had bought a scroll written by the famous Chin calligrapher Wang Hsi-chih]; Hsi-t'ang 溪堂, "The Hall near the brook"; and Ying-kuang-t'ang 英光堂, which probably stands for *shan-ying-lin-kuang* 山英林光, "Glory of the mountains and splendour of the wood." Other literary names refer to his official position: Nan-kung 南宮, which alludes to the place he occupied in the Li-pu 禮部, Board of Rites, and at the same time intimates literary brilliancy; and Huo-chêng-hou-jên 火正後人, 火正 being an old official title. The greater part of his literary names refer to localities: thus, Mi Hsiang-yang 米襄陽, for example, points to the place where his family lived, Hsiang-yang in Hupei province; and Lu-mên-chü-shih 鹿門居士, "The hermit of Lu-mên Mountain," refers to a mountain in Hsiang-yang-hsien, where, according to tradition, the elixir of immortality was to be found. He also called himself Hsiang-yang-man-shih 襄陽漫仕, "The vagrant officer of Hsiang-yang." The old name of Hupei was Ch'u 楚, so Mi Fu also styled himself Ch'u-kuo-mi-fu 楚國米黻, and Yü-hsiung-hou-jên 鬻熊後人, "The descendant of Yü Hsiung" (the founder of Ch'u). Further he called himself Huai-yang-wai-shih 淮陽外史, "The petty official of Huai-yang," Huai-yang being the place of his last official post, and where he died. The name Hsiang-mo-man-shih 相陌漫士 mentioned in Giles' Biographical Dictionary, sub No. 1530, I have not yet met with in Chinese sources, so I give it here as being subject to reserve.

The pronunciation of the character 芾 is discussed under the year 1091 (元祐六年辛未); for in this year Mi Fu, who up till then had always signed himself Mi Fu 米黻, began to use instead the characters 米芾. As 米芾 is the most widely used of his names in Chinese literature, in western books his name is written mostly with the character 芾, and not 黻. This character 芾 however, is sometimes transcribed *fei*, sometimes *fu*. As this transcription question supplies us with an important clue for determining the genuineness of Mi Fu's signature, I think it worth while to give here Wêng Fang-kang's discussion of the problem. He says: "Moreover I find that Mi in writing the character 芾 first drew a horizontal line, which subsequently he crossed by a straight perpendicular stroke, drawn from the top downwards. The lower part of this character 芾 follows 巿, pronounced *fu*. So this *fu* is the character 芾, and it has nothing to do with the character 市 as occurring in expressions like *chao-shih*, a morning market [cf. *Li-chi* 禮記, 郊特牲, 19], which is written with first a dot and then a horizontal line. All scrolls attributed to Mi on which this character is erroneously written with a dot and a horizontal line, adding *shih* 'market' to the radical for grass [the 140th radical 艹], are falsifications. Further I find that Mi used for his name first 黻 and afterwards 芾. As both characters are pronounced alike, viz. *fu*, he used on his chüan-style seal the character 亞[1], which means: two 己 back to back" (*Nien-pu*, page 8 recto: 又按米書芾字中間，先作一橫，然後自上以直畫貫下。此芾字下从巿，分勿切。巿即芾字。與朝市之市先上點而後橫畫者迥別。凡米蹟此字誤作一點一橫艹頭下加市井之市者，皆僞作也。又按米公名先寫黻，後寫芾。蓋以二字皆分勿切，故其印篆作亞，所謂兩已相背也。)

Thus the confusion in the transcription is caused by the fact that there are two different characters, 芾 *fu* and 芾 *fei*, which can be distinguished only by a minor detail, viz. the way in which the lower part is written. The first way is 一丨𠃌丨, where this lower part is pronounced *fu* (分付切), and which is used, with or without the

[1] This character was explained by Kuo P'o 郭璞 (276-324) in his commentary on the *Erh-ya* 爾雅 as "two 己 back to back"; it means a certain motive in embroidery. Perhaps, among other reasons, Mi Fu was induced to adopt the character 芾, because it recalled a variant of his family-name 米, viz. 芈 (cf. *S.K.*, ch. 124, under *Hua-shih*).

140th radical, as a variant of 黻, interchanged with 韍, and meaning "knee-cover." On the other hand, it may be written with five strokes 丶 一 丨 𠃌 丨, and it is then pronounced *shih* (石 矣 切), and means "market"; with the 140th radical on top this character is pronounced *fei*, and means "luxuriant vegetation." When we investigate the manuscripts of Mi Fu, we find that all the genuine scrolls show the character as 芾 written according to the first way (*v.* figs. I and II), which is only natural, since this character is a variant of his original name 黻. So in my opinion we should always transcribe the name 米 芾 Mi Fu, and not Mi Fei, or Mi Fu (Fei), for *Fu* is the only correct transcription.[1]

[1] The current Japanese pronunciation of Mi Fu is also *Bei Futsu.*

CHAPTER II

THE CHINESE INKSLAB AND THE *YEN-SHIH*

Before passing to the translation of the *Yen-shih*, it seems appropriate to make some general remarks on the material treated therein.

One of the most endearing features of the Chinese is their reverent love of all things pertaining to literature, and especially of writing and writing-materials. In the course of the many centuries during which the arts of calligraphy and "literary painting" (*shih-fu-hua* 士夫畫) were cherished and cultivated by a long line of ardent and talented scholars, scores of rules with their unavoidable exceptions were gradually evolved regarding the making and keeping of the various requisites of these arts. These rules were examined and re-examined with the utmost care, and then handed down in their final form from one scholar to another. So ink, inkslab, brush and paper, became at last those extremely refined implements that are known as *wên-fang-ssû-pao* 文房四寶, the "Four precious things of the library."

With the stick of ink one rubs the inkslab, then the brush is moistened, and the paper lies ready to receive the columns of graceful characters, or the few expressive strokes that evoke, as if by magic, the very essence of a scene from nature. After some time, however, the stick of ink gets rubbed down to a mere stub, and one has to choose a new one. The hairs of the brush, too, become frayed, and generally after the lapse of one year it cannot be used any longer. So the only thing that remains constant, after all, is the ink-stone. It will last for years and years, and even for centuries. No wonder that of the four precious things the inkslab (*yen* 硯, 研, modern colloquial *yen-t'ai* 硯臺) has always been valued most highly by calligraphers and connoisseurs.

Many treatises on ink-stones were written, in which their faults and merits, their shapes and colours, their places of origin and prices were discussed at length To this class belongs Mi Fu's book, the *Yen-shih*, or "An Account of Ink-stones." Though consisting of only one chapter, it has always been considered as an authoritative work, and accordingly it is extensively quoted in later books on ink-stones, and in dictionaries and works of reference generally. This treatise is to be found in various *ts'ung-shu*. The editions differ only in minor details—for the most part the various readings are due to obvious mistakes on the part of the men who carved the blocks.

The oldest and best text is given in the *ts'ung-shu* of the Sung dynasty entitled *Pai-ch'uan-hsüeh-hai* 百川學海, published by Ts'o Kuei 左圭 (style: Yü-hsi 禹錫), preface dated 1273.

Further, it is to be found in the huge *ts'ung-shu* of the end of the Yüan dynasty, the *Shuo-fu* 說郛, compiled by T'ao Tsung-i 陶宗儀 (style: Chiu-ch'êng 九成; born *circa* 1320). A description of this collection is given in *S.K.*, ch. 123; cf., however, the detailed discussion by P. Pelliot in *T'oung Pao*, vol. XXIII, pp. 163 *sq*. In referring to this edition I use *S.F.*

It is also contained in the Ming *ts'ung-shu*: *Ch'ün-fang-ch'ing-wan* 羣芳清玩 (referred to as *C.F.C.W.*), a small collection compiled by Li Yü 李璵 (style: Hui-shih 惠時). This edition claims to represent a redaction by Mao Chin (cf. p. 3); but as it abounds in mistakes, this statement is to be considered suspect.

Another Ming edition of our text is to be found in the *Mi-hsiang-yang-chih-lin*, the compilation published by Fan Ming-t'ai (*v. supra* p. 4). This text was revised by two scholars: Li Ch'iao 李翹, about whom I have been unable to find any details, and Wang Hsia 王洽 (style: Ho-chung 和仲), an official who became *chin-shih* 進士 during the Wan-li period (1573-1619). This edition I refer to as *F.Y.S.*

The *Yen-shih* is also contained in the *ts'ung-shu* of the Chia-ch'ing 嘉慶 period (1796-1820), entitled *Hsüeh-chin-t'ao-yüan* 學津討原 and published by Chang Hai-p'êng 張海鵬 (referred to as *H.C. T.Y.*).

Finally, it is to be found in the two recent *ts'ung-shu* mentioned above, the *Hu-pei-hsien-chêng-i-shu*, which gives a photographic reprint of the text in the *Pai-ch'uan-hsüeh-hai*, and the *Mei-shu-ts'ung-shu*, referred to as *M.S.T.S.* I used the second edition of 1928, where the *Yen-shih* is to be found in the fourth collection, III, 4. The first edition (1910) reproduces the text as published in the *Hsüeh-chin-t'ao-yüan* (see above).

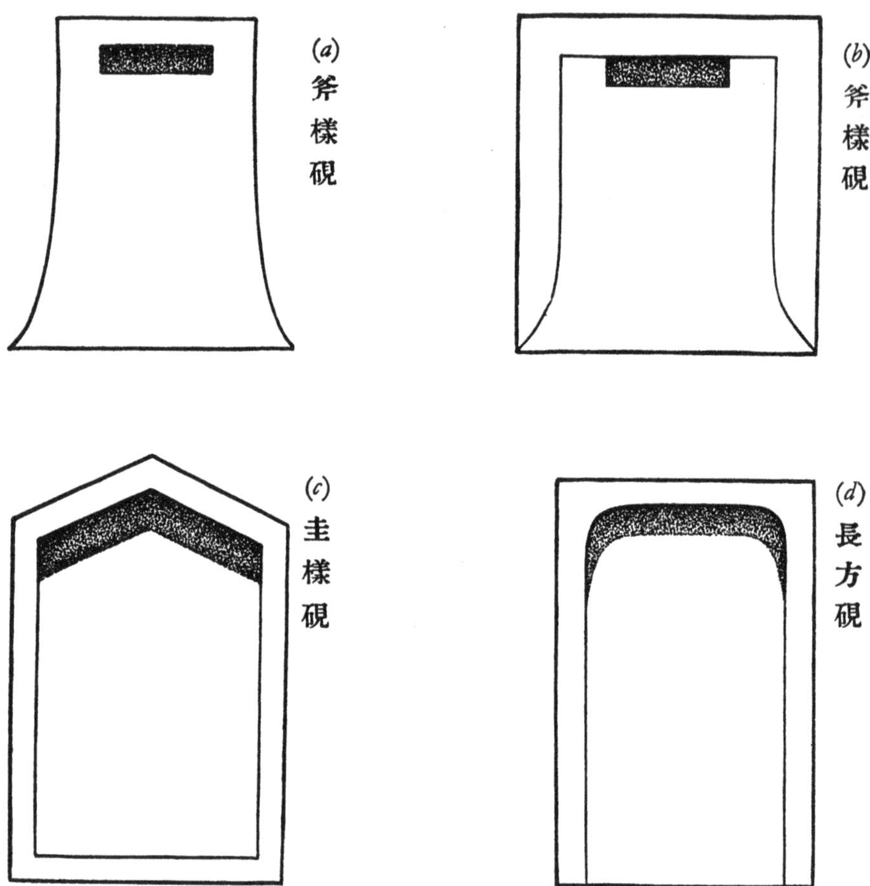

SOME COMMON TYPES OF INKSLABS

(*a*) *Fu-yang-yen*, inkslab in the shape of an axe. The rectangular cavity contains the pure water, the ink is rubbed on the surface below.

(*b*) Same as (*a*). The surface where the ink is rubbed is in the shape of an axe.

(*c*) *Kuei-yang-yen*, in the shape of an ancient jade-tablet, a symbol of authority, granted by the Emperor.

(*d*) *Ch'ang-fang-yen*, oblong square slab, the usual form in which ink-stones are carved.

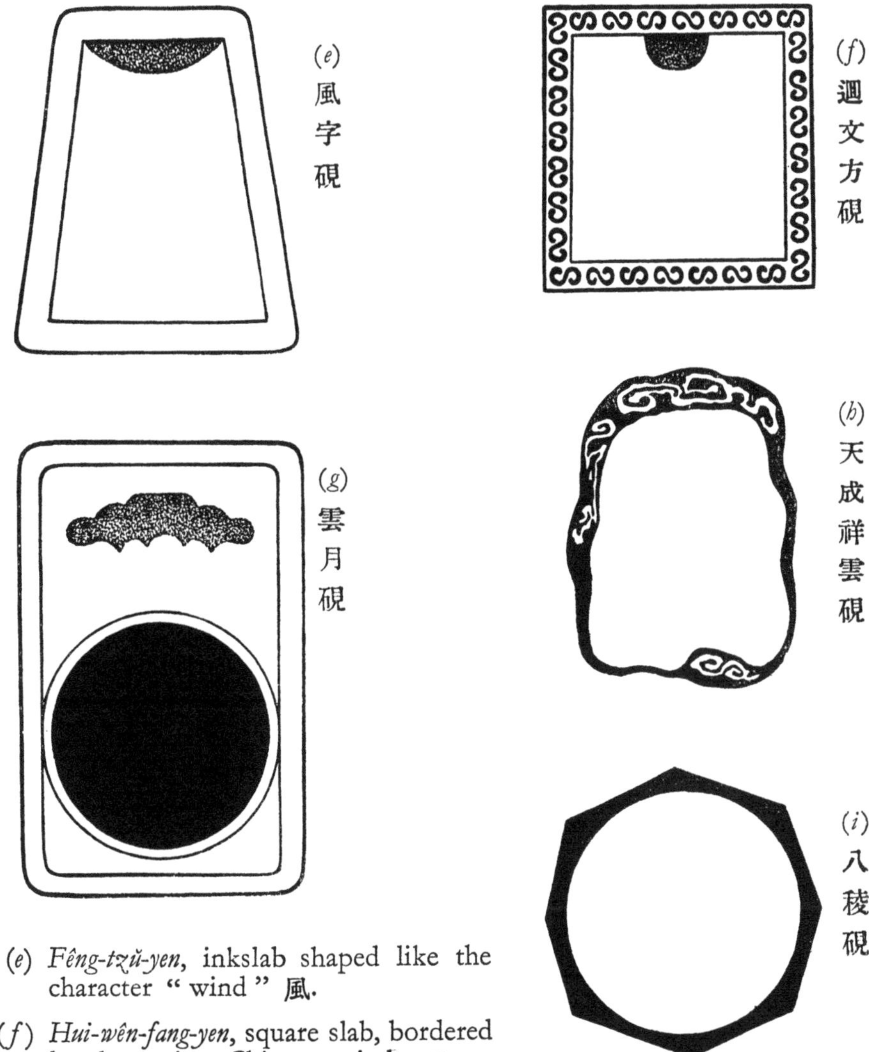

(*e*) *Fêng-tzŭ-yen*, inkslab shaped like the character " wind " 風.

(*f*) *Hui-wên-fang-yen*, square slab, bordered by the ancient Chinese spiral pattern.

(*g*) *Yün-yüeh-yen*, inkslab showing clouds and the moon. The cavity on top, shaped like a cloud, contains the pure water, and the ink is rubbed on the round face, which represents the moon.

(*h*) *T'ien-ch'êng-hsiang-yün-yen*, an ink-stone which is naturally shaped like auspicious clouds.

(*i*) *Pa-lêng-yen*, eight-cornered ink-stone. Often the eight triagrams *pa-kua* 八卦 are to be found depicted on the eight sides.

My translation is based on the text of the *Pai-ch'uan-hsüeh-hai*, which I reprint below. For the sake of completeness I have added the different readings of the other editions in foot-notes to the Chinese text, marked *a*, *b*, etc.

The scholars who have edited this difficult text seem to have contented themselves with making some insignificant alterations; and the passages where the meaning is most obscure they leave untouched. Further, no edition is punctuated, so I have ventured to perform this risky task myself. Not without reason indeed it is said in Mi Fu's biography in the *Sung-shih* 宋史 (ch. 444) that "in his literary work Mi Fu was weird and reckless, not treading in the tracks of the ancients" (芾為文奇險, 不蹈襲前人軌轍).

Of his predecessors in this field Mi Fu mentions Su I-chien 蘇易簡 (style: T'ai-chien 太簡; 958-996), the author of a general work on writing-materials, the *Wên-fang-ssû-pu* 文房四譜, in which the second chapter, *Yen-pu* 硯譜, is devoted to ink-stones. I have used the edition of the *Shih-wan-chüan-lou-ts'ung-shu* 十萬卷樓叢書, edited in 1879 by Lu Hsin-yüan 陸心源 (style: Kang-fu 剛甫, 1834-1894); and secondly the text as given in the *Hsüeh-hai-lei-pien* 學海類編 edited by Ts'ao Ch'iu-yo 曹秋岳 in the Tao-kuang period (1821-1850). In my concluding chapter I shall compare the plan and merits of this work with the treatise of Mi Fu.

Mi Fu also cites another small book, called *Hsi-chou-yen-t'u* 歙州硯圖, "The ink-stones of Hsi-chou, with illustrations," and written by an unknown author. A colophon bears the date of 1066. In catalogues this book is quoted under the title *Hsi-chou-yen-pu* 歙州硯譜; and the reason for the change is that in the *Pai-ch'uan-hsüeh-hai*, the oldest edition, the editor thought it too expensive to publish the illustrations, which consequently have been lost [cf. the discussion in *S.K.*, ch. 115, page 4 recto].

Finally Mi Fu quotes from T'ang Hsün 唐詢 (style: Yen-yu 彥猷; *chin-shih* 進士 between 1023-31; *v. Sung-shih* 宋史, ch. 303), who composed a treatise on ink-stones in three chapters, called *Yen-lu* 硯錄.

It seems that in or about Mi Fu's period the study of ink-stones was very popular, for several essays on this subject appeared.

The scholar Chu Ch'ang-wên 朱長文 (style: Po-yüan 伯原; 1041-1100) in his *Mo-ch'ih-pien* 墨池編 (preface dated 1066) made a special study of the ink-stone (*v.* ch. 19), and embodied in it the text of T'ang Hsün's book and the greater part of Su I-chien's chapter on ink-stones.

The famous scholar Ou-yang Hsiu 歐陽修 (style: Yung-shu 永叔; 1007-1072) also wrote a *Yen-pu* 硯譜 (in his complete works, 外集, ch. 25), where he cites T'ang Hsün, Su I-chien, and Ts'ai Hsiang (*v. infra*).

Ou-yang Hsiu, T'ang Hsün and Su I-chien are quoted in another *Yen-pu* 硯譜, by an unknown author. This *Yen-pu*, and the following two treatises, are to be found in the *Pai-ch'uan-hsüeh-hai*.

The *Tuan-hsi-yen-pu* 端溪硯譜 is especially devoted to the Tuan-hsi stones. Its author is unknown, but according to a colophon it must have been written *circa* 1145.

The *Hsi-yen-shuo* 歙硯說 treats chiefly of stones from Hsi-chou. Its author is unknown. It quotes T'ang Hsün and Su I-chien.

The scholar Yeh Mêng-tê 葉夢得 (style: Shao-yün 少蘊; 1077-1147) made some remarks on ink-stones in his *Pi-shu-lu-hua* 避暑錄話 [in the 汲古閣 edition: 上卷, page 18-19, 下卷, pages 22 and 62], where he quotes from Mi Fu.

T'ang Hsün is also quoted by his friend Ts'ai Hsiang 蔡襄 (style: Chün-mo 君謨; 1012-1067), in his *Wên-fang-ssû-shuo* 文房四說 [蔡忠惠公集, published 1615, chapter 34], where he discusses several sorts of ink-stones. The same author composed also a very brief *Yen-chi* 硯記 [*ibid.*, ch. 34], dated 1053.

Posterior to Mi Fu is Kao Ssŭ-sun 高似孫 (style: Hsü-ku 續古), who wrote the *Yen-chien* 硯箋, a book in four chapters, and in which the books mentioned above are all extensively quoted. The preface is dated 1223. Unfortunately the illustrations that belonged to this book have been lost.

It is not necessary to attempt here an enumeration of all the countless books on ink-stones composed by the scholars of subsequent dynasties. Few of them present the results of independent research, their contents for the most part being nothing but a repetition of the statements of the older authors mentioned above. Some of the more original ones, which I have consulted while translating the *Yen-shih*, I may briefly describe here.

(*a*) *Yen-lin* 硯林, "The Forest of ink-stones," by Yü Huai 余懷 (style: Tan-hsin 澹心, also Wu-huai 無懷, born in 1617). Yü Huai was much praised as a poet, and he was known as an ardent collector of ink-stones. In his preface to the *Yen-lin* he says that his book is nothing more than an elaboration of Mi Fu's *Yen-shih;* nevertheless, it contains much new material.

(*b*) *Pao-yen-t'ang-yen-pien* 寶硯堂硯辨, "Discussions on ink-stones from the Hall where ink-stones are treasured," by Ho Ch'uan-yao 何傳瑤, published in 1837. A rare item, authoritative for Tuan-hsi stones. The scholar Huang P'ei-fang 黃培芳 added two maps of the Tuan quarries.

(*c*) *Tuan-hsi-yen-shih* 端溪硯史, "Account of the Tuan-hsi stones," by Wu Lan-hsiu 吳蘭修 (style: Shih-hua 石華), preface dated 1834. This book, although chiefly devoted to the Tuan-hsi stones, may be considered as the most comprehensive work on the subject of ink-stones in general. The author frequently quotes Mi Fu's book, as well as (*a*) and (*b*). He gives five maps of the sites of the quarries.

Some of the later books also contain drawings of ink-stones, with short descriptions. I mention here, e.g., the *Wên-fang-ssû-k'ao* 文房肆考, by T'ang Ping-chün 唐秉鈞, preface dated 1776, where much care is given to the reproduction of the decorations and inscriptions of the stones. A series of drawings of forty famous ink-stones (among which is Mi Fu's favourite earthenware inkslab, in the shape of a falcon) is found in various collections and reference-works, e.g., in the huge collection *Ku-chin-t'u-shu-chi-ch'êng* 古今圖書集成. There exist also numerous collections of rubbings, taken from ink-stones, and reproducing their shapes and inscriptions.

The most comprehensive work on the various shapes of ink-stones is doubtless the splendid Imperial collection *Hsi-ch'ing-yen-pu* 西清硯譜. Hsi-ch'ing was another name for the South Library, Nan-shu-fang 南書房 in the northern part of the Forbidden City, to the west of the Ch'ien-ch'ing-mên 乾清門. The preface is dated 1778.

This book in 25 chapters carefully reproduces all the stones of the Imperial collections as seen from various angles, and moreover it gives dates and inscriptions, to which are added eulogies on the stones written by the Imperial brush. A good photographic reproduction has been published by the Commercial Press, Shanghai.

From this book we can form an idea of the astounding variety of shapes of ink-stones. Practically every motive of Chinese mythology, every emblem of Chinese symbolism is found expressed in the decoration of the ink-stone, which has become a finished product of fine art.

None of these illustrations, however, gives us an idea of the colour and grain of the various sorts of stone, elements which are very important in judging an ink-stone. The only book that gives excellent pictures of ink-stones in their natural colours is, as far as I know, the *Seikakenfu* 精華硯譜, a collection of coloured pictures of ink-stones, with short descriptions, published by Yugawa Genyō 湯川元洋, Ōsaka 1917.

Last year there was published in Japan a very detailed study of ink-stones and ink, *Gemboku-shingo* 硯墨新語, "New discussions on ink-stones and ink," by Iijima Shigeru 飯島茂, Tōkyō 1935. In more than 500 amply illustrated pages the author discusses Japanese and Chinese ink-stones, giving the literary sources and supplementing these by modern mineralogical methods; he analyses the various kinds of stone and ink microscopically, and records the results in interesting tables. The sinological data, however, leave much to be desired, since his references are often wrong, and his Japanese translations of Chinese texts are very arbitrary. Still it is an interesting study, and, as far as I know, the only modern scientific book on the subject.

Good reproductions of ink-stones are given in a small booklet which appeared in February 1936, *Kokenbi-no-kanshō* 古硯美の鑑賞, by Inoue Genta 井上源太.

In Ōsaka in September 1936, Inoue Seiichi 井上清一 published a brief but very informative treatise on Tuan-hsi inkslabs, called *Senkenroku* 洗硯錄;—here also some good reproductions of old Chinese ink-stones are given.

In these books about ink-stones and the stones from which they are made, a number of special technical terms are used. Most of them cannot be found in any dictionary, and my renderings are therefore more or less guess-work, based upon the context. Although I have tried to verify them by comparing the literary data with actual stones in private collections and curio-shops, they by no means pretend to be final.

The ordinary inkslab is divided into an upper and a lower part. The upper part is called *yen-t'ou* 硯頭, and here is a cavity, filled with pure water for moistening the stone before rubbing the ink. This depression is called *yen-ch'ih* 硯池, or *shui-ch'ih* 水池. The lower part of the stone is formed by the flat surface on which the ink is to be rubbed. This place is called *mo-ch'ih* 墨池 or *mo-ch'u* 墨處; also *yen-ch'ih* 硯池 just like the upper part. While one is rubbing the ink, several things may happen. For instance, one feels the stick of ink slip—it does not 'grip' the stone; then the stone is called *hua* 滑, 'slippery.' This will occur when the stone has been rubbed too much, and consequently has become 'tired,' *fa* 乏; or when the stone has been touched with greasy fingers; or simply because the stone is naturally very hard and smooth. In this case it will take more time than usual before the three constitutents of good ink, viz. water, ink, and the fine dust ground off the stone by rubbing, mix to "produce the ink," *fa-mo* 發墨. Then the stone is called 'slow,' *man* 慢, in contradistinction from 'quick,' *k'uai* 快 stones, which produce ink in a short time. Some stones "repel the ink," *chü-mo-chê* 拒墨者, that is to say, the ink mixes with the water, but not with the stone itself, with the result that the ink becomes 'shallow,' *tan* 淡. The opposite of *chü-mo-chê* is *cho-mo-chê* 著墨者, said of those stones that 'grip' the ink. When the ink is being rubbed, some very porous stones will absorb the ink, so that it soon dries up. This is a bad quality in an ink-stone, a fault that is called 'absorbing,' *shên* 滲. In judging an ink-stone, attention is also given to the colour and the sound. The sound of a stone is tested by suspending it on a hook and rapping it with the knuckle of the finger.

Very important, finally, is the *shih-li* 石理, the grain or texture of the stone. When the grain is too hard, the place where the ink is rubbed will, after being used for some time, become uneven, and chips will be knocked off the stick of ink. Stones with a good grain will, on the contrary, facilitate the movement of rubbing. Important are also the 'markings,' the pattern of the stone. These markings are called *wên* 紋 when they run parallel to one another, and *lo-wên* 羅紋 when they run criss-cross.

Other terms which occur only two or three times in the *Yen-shih* will be explained in the annotations to the text.

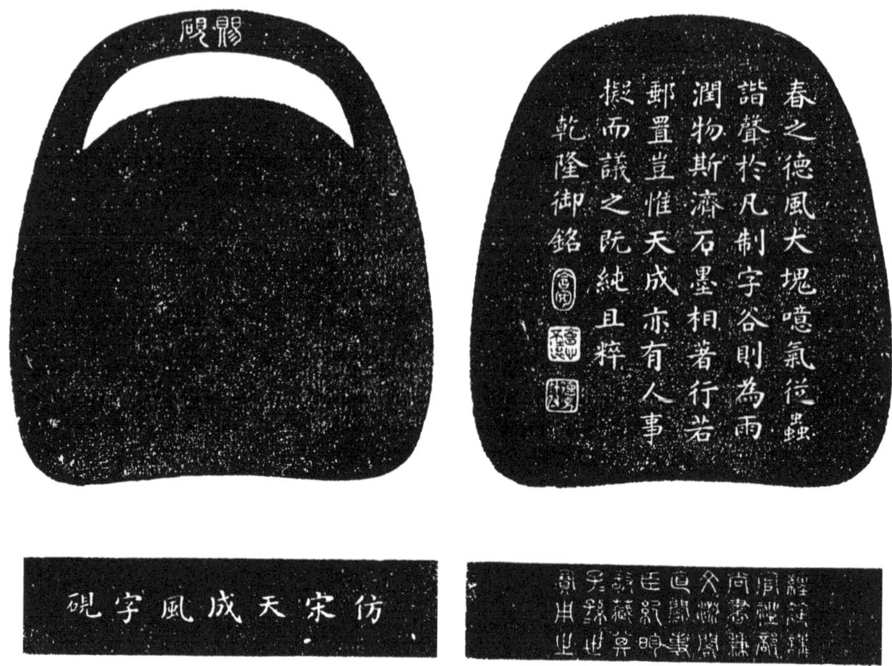

'WIND' CHARACTER INK-STONE, *Fêng-tzû-yen* 風字硯
(Collection of Chi Yün)

On top are written the two characters *ssû-yen* 賜硯, "Ink-stone granted by the Emperor."

The inscription on the frontside runs, "Ink-stone naturally shaped like the character *fêng* 風 (wind), in imitation of a Sung stone."

THE INSCRIPTION on the reverse runs: "A breeze is the great virtue of spring; it is, as the philosopher Chuang-tzû observed, like a long-drawn, sad sigh. The word "wind" (*fêng*) rhymes with the word "insect" (*ch'ung*). Placing the character "insect" inside the character *fan* (凡), the character "wind" is formed. When rain falls in the vale, all things are purified (this refers to the moistening of the ink-slab). When the stick of ink and the stone touch each other, the ink will be produced with the swiftness of post-couriers. This is not only due to the natural qualities of the stone, but also to the work of man. With such thoughts in my mind I composed these lines (praising) the purity (of this stone) and its fine quality.

Written by the Emperor Ch'ien-lung."

THE INSCRIPTION in seal-characters runs: 經筵講官禮部尚書兼文淵閣直閣事臣紀昀敬藏。其子孫世寶用之.

"Reverently stored away by Chi Yün, official who explains the Classics to the Emperor, President of the Board of Rites, and official on duty at the Wên-yüan Library. May his children and grandchildren use and treasure it, for many generations to come."

NOTE:—The Wên-yüan-ko (also called Ssû-k'u) was built by Ch'ien-lung. The vast Imperial collection of books was housed there, and the descriptive catalogue thereof was drawn up under direction of Chi Yün. The last sentence of the inscription is the conventional phrase taken from ancient sacrificial tripods.

CHAPTER III

" AN ACCOUNT OF INK-STONES "

I.—Introduction [1]

人[a]好萬殊，而以甚同爲公，甚不同爲惑。喻之而移，非眞得[b]之。更而得之，則必信其守。夫博弈由[c]賢乎已，則吾是文必不見嗤於賞鑒之士。

Peoples' tastes are widely different; but that which is liked by the great mass is considered to be right, whilst that which is liked only by a few (e.g., the collecting of ink-stones) is considered to be cranky. But when one can be persuaded to abandon one's hobby, one is not really devoted to it; for when one is really devoted to it, one will be sure to persevere in it. As Confucius said [2] that even to be a gamester or a chess-player is still better than doing nothing at all, this little book of mine should not be laughed at by discriminating [3] scholars.[4]

Annotations. [1] In none of the texts are the paragraphs numbered. For convenience's sake, however, I have treated here each separate passage as a chapter, marked with a Roman number.—[2] Cf. *Lun-yü* 論語, XVII, 22: The Master said: " Hard is the case of him, who will stuff himself with food the whole day, without applying his mind to anything good! Are there not gamesters and chess-players? To be one of these would still be better than doing nothing at all " (Legge).—[3] The term *shang-chien*, explained as *shang-shih-chien-pieh* 賞識鑒別, " to rejoice in appraising and to investigate critically (cf. *Tz'ŭ-yüan* 辭源, s.v.) seems to have been coined by Mi Fu. He uses this term of the way a cultured, true lover of art will choose and pore over his treasures, in contradistinction from the ignorant amateur (*hao-shih-chê* 好事者), who buys at random what he likes at first

---

a. *H. C. T. Y.* reads *liao* 療, making the meaning of the first sentence something like: " The ways in which people try to appease their craving for a hobby are widely different "; I think, however, that the reading *jên* is the better and probably the original one.

b. *H. C. T. Y.* reads *jên* 人, which makes a clumsy sentence, and moreover introduces a word with a Taoist flavour (眞人) in a text which belongs decidedly to the Ju-class, 儒家.

c. All other texts read *yu* 猶, which brings the quotation closer to the *Lun-yü* passage, which also has 猶.

sight in order to form a big collection, without being able really to enjoy the beauty of things. The disdain with which Mi Fu viewed the latter class appears from ironical remarks of his, such as : " Those among people to-day who love strange things..." (v. below, chapter VI, sixth paragraph) ; "...for those (people) who consider strangeness as a superior quality (in an ink-stone)..." (v. below, chapter VII, second paragraph) ; " ... amateurs who only attach value to things as curios... (v. below, chapter XXIII). The term *shang-chien* is used extensively by later writers on art. As *shōkan* (*suru*) it found its way into the Japanese artistic vocabulary.—[4] This brief and very pregnant introduction is evidently meant to be a pendant to Su I-chien's epilogue to his *Wên-fang-ssû-pu*. Here we find the same idea expressed in other words. This epilogue reads :

班志有言曰小說家流千三百八十篇,蓋出於稗官道塗之說也。孔子曰小道亦有可觀者焉苟致遠而不泥庶亦幾於道也。矧善其事者必利其器,尋其波者必討其源。吾見其決洩古先之道,發揚翰墨之精,莫不由是四者。方傳之無窮乎。苟闕其一雖敏妙之士,如廉頗不能將楚人也。嘗觀茶經竹譜尚言始末成一家之說。況世爲儒者,焉能無述哉。因閱書祕府遂檢尋前志幷耳目所及交知所載者集成此譜。問之通識者,識者亦曰可。故不能棄。其冠序則有右騎省徐公述焉。敢以胸臆之志復書於卷末云。

" Pan Ku (A.D. 32-92) said in his *I-wên-chih :* The writings of the *Hsiao-shuo* class fill 1,380 volumes [Su I-chien copies the misprint in the original ; loc. cit. 1,390 vols. are enumerated] ; they originated from the talk of petty officials, and from gossip in the dirt of the road. Confucius (properly : Tzŭ-hsia) said : Even in inferior studies and employments there is something worth being looked at [Legge, *Lun-yü*, XIX, 4 ; the text then goes on : 致遠恐泥, " but if they are carried through to more remote things, one risks to become stuck in the mud." Su I-chien connects this 泥 with the 塗 of the quotation from Pan Ku, and works out the idea as follows]. If one pursues the study (of inferior and trifling things) further, without, however, becoming stuck in the mud, does one not then come near to the real Way ? Moreover, if one wishes to accomplish one's work, one should first sharpen one's tools [cf. *Lun-yü*, XV, 9] ; when one wishes to investigate the waves, one should go back as far as the source [quoted from *Wên-hsüan* 文選, ch. 4, 陸士衡文賦 : 沿波討源]. Now I find that the ways of the ancients are made apparent, and the essence of literature propagated, solely by means of these four things [referring to the title of his book : inkslab, brush, ink and paper]. Only these four things cause tradition to flow on unbroken. If one of them is missing, even the cleverest and most wonderful scholar is in the same predicament as Lien P'o, who could not lead the people of Ch'u to victory [Lien P'o was a famous general of the Warring States period ; his exploits are described in his biography in the *Shih-chi* 史記, ch. 81. When in his later years he went to Ch'u, he was not able, inspite of his skill as a strategist, to gain any victory]. Now I have seen that the Book of Tea [by Lu Yü 陸羽, died 804] and the Book of Bamboo [by Tai K'ai-chih 戴凱之, Chin 晉 period], treating their subjects in great detail, have risen to be considered as forming each a class of its own. How much less then could the things by which the literati of this world exist be left without record? Therefore I perused the books in the Imperial library, searched through old records: combining this with what I heard and saw, and with what was brought forward by my friends and acquaintances, I compiled this book. I asked some wise men for their opinion, and they approved of it, so I did not abandon it. The first preface was written by the head of the San-ch'i-shêng [a kind of documentary section] Hsü Hsüan 徐鉉 (916-991). Now at the end of the book I myself venture to express here my sincere thoughts."

Following the editor of the *Hsüeh-hai-lei-pien*, I take the above to be an epilogue. The editor of the *Shih-wan-chüan-lou-ts'ung-shu* makes it a preface, *hsü* 序, and inserts it directly after the preface of Hsü Hsüan; he takes the last sentence to mean something like: "I shall venture to speak my mind a second time (復) at the end of this book." This epilogue referred to, however, is missing. I therefore prefer to follow the editor of the *Hsüeh-hai-lei-pien*, and take 復 to refer to the fact that as such an eminent scholar as Hsü Hsüan had already written a preface, an epilogue is, properly speaking, superfluous.

II.—On the Use of Ink-stones

用品。器以用爲功。玉不爲鼎，陶不爲柱。文錦之美，方暑則不先於表出之絺。楮葉雖工，而無補於宋人之用。夫如是，則石理發墨爲上，色次之，形製工拙又其次。文藻緣飾，雖天然，失硯之用。

The merit of an implement depends on its being usable. Of jade one does not make sacrificial tripods, of earthenware one does not make pillars. The beauty of embroidered garments is, during the heat of summer, of no more use than a coat of plain cloth.[1] A mulberry-leaf, however finely carved (out of jade), is of no use to the people of Sung.[2] In just the same way the grain of the stone and the producing of ink are the main things; the colour comes next, and least important are the shape and quality of the workmanship. Ornate pattern and adornment, though they may be inherent in the stone, have nothing to do with the true purpose of an ink-stone.

Annotations. [1] Cf. *Lun-yü*, X, 6.—[2] Refers to an anecdote of Lieh-tzû 列子: A man of Sung had worked for three years on carving an exact likeness of a mulberry-leaf out of jade. Put among real leaves, it was not distinguishable from them. When Lieh-tzû heard of it, he said tartly: "If Nature needed three years to make one leaf, there would indeed be very few things with leaves!" The meaning is that the real nature of things is the only thing that matters, and painstaking detail-work is not important. A finely carved ink-stone is inferior to a plain square slab that quickly produces good ink.

III.—Ink-stones of Jade

玉硯。玉出光爲硯，著墨不滲。甚發墨有光。其云磨墨處不出光者，非也。余自製成蒼玉硯。

If one makes ink-stones of shining jade, they will grip the ink without absorbing it. They will abundantly produce shining ink. Those who say that the spot where one rubs the inkstick does not shine, are wrong. I myself made an ink-stone of greenish jade.[1]

Annotation. [1] *Ts'ang-yü* seems to be a special kind of jade, mentioned also in other books on ink-stones. The assertion which Mi Fu contests here was made by the T'ang painter Li Fang-shu, 李方叔 (quoted in the *Yen-chien* of Kao Ssû-sun, ch. 3).

IV.—Stones from the Rock of Ko-hsien-kung[1] at Fang-ch'êng-hsien, T'ang-chou[2]

唐州方城縣葛仙公巖石。石理向日視之，如玉瑩，如鑑光，而著墨，如澄泥，不滑。稍磨之墨已下，而不熱生泡。生泡者膠也。古墨無泡，膠力盡也。若石[a]滑，磨久墨下遲，則兩剛生熱，故膠生泡也。此石[b]既不熱，良久墨發，生光如漆如油。有艶不滲也。歲久不乏，常如新成。有君子一德之操。色紫可愛，聲平而有韻。亦有澹清白色，如月，如星而無暈。此石近出，始[c]見十餘枚矣。

The grain of this stone is such, that when one looks at it in the light of the sun, it is resplendent like jade, and brilliant like a mirror: but it grips the ink, for it is like (an inkslab) of pure clay, and it does not become slippery. When rubbed only a little, the ink comes down, without producing any heat or bubbles. If bubbles come up, they are caused by the glue (in the inkstick). Old inksticks do not produce bubbles, because the force of the glue in them is

---

a. *C.F.C.W.* reads 墨, and for b. 若; both are evidently misprints.

c. *C.F.C.W.* reads 如, evidently a misprint.

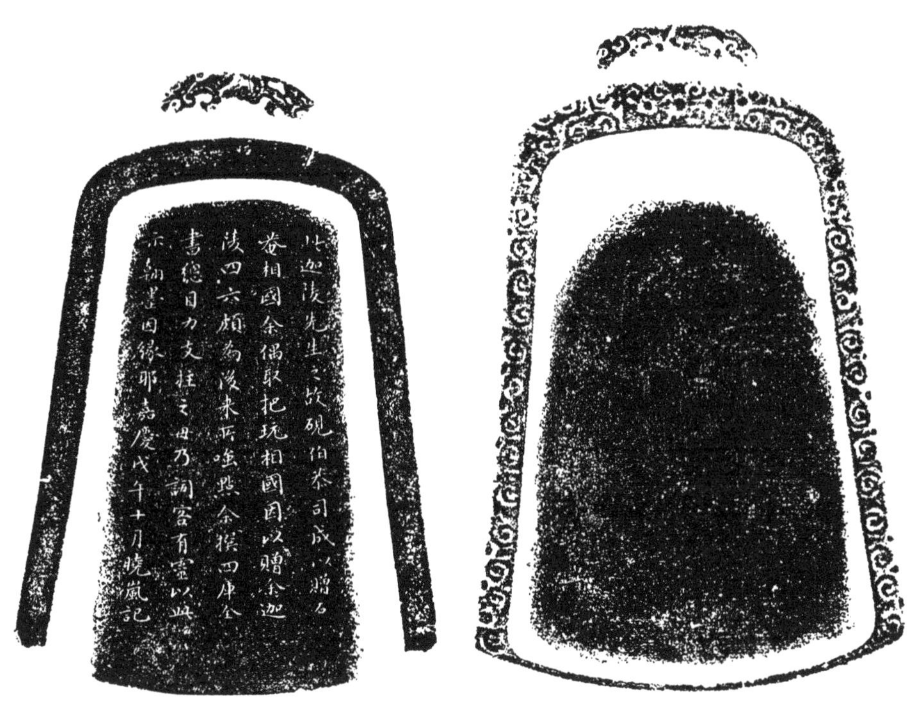

Ink-stone in the Shape of a Bell, *Chung-yang-yen* 鐘樣硯
(Collection of Chi Yün)

Inscription: "This is an old stone from the collection of Ch'ên Wei-sung 陳維崧 (style: Chi-nien 其年, literary name Chia-ling, 1625-1682). The Libationer in the Imperial Academy, Ch'ên Ch'ung-pên 陳崇本 (literary name Po-kung), gave it to the Prime Minister Liu Yung 劉墉 (literary name Shih-an, 1719-1803). Once I happened to contemplate this stone, and the Prime Minister presented it to me. Scholars of later times have much ridiculed Ch'ên Wei-sung on account of his bad poetical essays (*tz'û*). At the time that I composed the *Ssû-k'u-ch'üan-shu-tsung-mu*, however, I vindicated him vigorously (cf. *op. cit.*, chapter 65, page 6), and this inscription also tends to assert that he possessed the genius of a poet.

Written by Shao-lan, in the year 1798, the tenth month."

exhausted. If the stone is slippery, and the ink comes down slowly and only after rubbing a long time, heat will be produced by the contact of the two hard things (viz. the stone and the inkstick); and then the glue will produce bubbles. As this stone never becomes warm it will produce ink for a very long time. It shines like varnish, or like oil. It is beautiful, and it does not absorb. Even after many years it does not become tired; it will always remain like new. So thus it possesses the unvarying virtue[3] of the Superior Man: consistency. It has a lovely purple colour, and its sound is even and harmonious. There are also stones of a pale, whitish colour, like the moon, or like the stars, and without any stains. This stone was recently discovered; as yet I saw some ten specimens of it.

Annotations. [1] Ko Hsüan 葛玄, style Lao-hsien 老仙, was a Taoist recluse of the San-kuo period who tried to find the elixir of life. He was afterwards called Ko Hsien-kung.—[2] At present Fang-ch'êng-hsien 方城縣, Honan province.—[3] I-tê, cf. *Shu-ching* 書經, ed. Legge, IV: VI, 3, 4; cf. also *Shih-ching* 詩經, same ed., I: V, IV, 4; II, VIII, V, 7.

V.—Stones from the Rock near the Nunnery of the Avatamsaka School, at Wên-chou[1]

溫州華嚴尼寺巖石。石理向日視之如方城石。磨墨不熱無泡。發墨生光如漆如油。有艶不滲。色赤而多有白沙點，爲硯則避磨墨處。比方城差慢。難嶄而易磨。亦有白點，點處有玉性。扣之聲平無韻。校理石揚休所購王羲之硯者乃此石。今人所收古硯，間有此石。形合晉畫。約見四五枚矣。

The grain of this stone, when one looks at it in the light of the sun, is the same as that of the Fang-ch'êng stone (*v. supra*, ch. IV). When the ink is being rubbed, it does not become warm, nor does it produce bubbles. The ink it produces is brilliant like varnish or oil. It is beautiful and it does not absorb. Its colour is red, with many white, sandy spots; when making an inkslab of this kind of stone one should take care that these white spots do not occur on the place where the ink is to be rubbed. It does not produce ink as quickly as the Fang-ch'êng stone. It is difficult to hollow out, but easy to grind ink on. There are also stones with white spots. These spots have the nature of jade. If one knocks the stone, its sound is even but not harmonious. The inkslab of Wang Hsi-chih,[2] which was bought by the Archivist Shih Yang-hsiu,[3] was of this sort. This kind of stone is occasionally found among the old ink-stones preserved by contemporary collectors. Its shape is in accordance with those shown in the pictures of the Chin period. In all I have seen four or five pieces.

Annotations. [1] Yung-chia-hsien 永嘉縣, Chekiang province.—[2] Wang Hsi-chih, style: I-shao 逸少 (321-379), the paragon of all Chinese calligraphers. —[3] Shih Yang-hsiu, style: Ch'ang-yen 昌言. His biography in the *Sung-shih* 宋史, ch. 299, calls him *pi-ko-hsiao-li* 秘閣校理, Imperial Archivist. He was a famous *ch'in* 琴 player, who composed the well-known tune *Yüan-ho-shuang-ch'ing* 猿鶴雙清 (cf. the *Ch'in-pu-ho-pi-ta-ch'üan* 琴譜合璧大全, preface dated 1573, ch. 3).

VI.—Stones from the Rocks at Tuan-chou [1]

端州巖石。巖有四，下巖，上巖，半邊巖，後礫巖。余嘗至端，故得其說詳。

下巖第一。穿洞深入，不論四時，皆爲水浸。治平中貢硯取水月餘方及石。石細，扣之淸越。鸜鵒眼圓，碧暈多明瑩。石嫩甚者如泥，無聲，不著墨。淸越者溫潤，著墨快，不熱無泡。然良久微滲，若油發艶。亦有不乏者。然方城溫巖十磨此石三十磨方相及。下巖既深，工人所費多，硯直不補[a]，故力無能取，近年[b]無復有。聞有仁廟已前賜史院官硯多是。其後來歲貢惟上巖石。

上巖在山上。石性乾，紫色深。理粗，性硬。眼黃差不圓。而靑色淡。其巖深處，間有潤者而眼終不如下巖也。有著墨者，拒墨者。其著墨者初用半月前甚快，蓋細砂石所發出理也。半月後則退生光。撻墨又須以柔石發之已而復然。拒墨者雖新成便拒墨。此等石扣之聲皆堅響而老。

半邊巖者在山半。石理同上巖，色多靑紫近黑[c]。多瑕而眼長[d]如卵。有瞎眼者中是白點。死眼者黑點而暈。細翳眼者或靑或黑，橫亂其眼。又多靑不成眼，圓點橫長，靑間道如松木紋。其極粗者費筆而稍細者多乏。

後礫石土[e]人刻爲盋印合壓紙兒戲之物。多夾砂無眼少瑕。間有極細軟者。發墨不乏。扣之無聲。土人不貴而用實有在半邊上巖之上者，不可常得。

---

a. *S.F.* leaves out 補.

b. *S.F.* here inserts 補.

c. *C.F.C.W.* reads 墨, an evident misprint.

d. *C.F.C.W.* reads 大.

e. All texts have 上; I prefer, with *M.S.T.S.*, to read 土.

又徧詢石工云子石未嘗有。其在巖中實。於大石版上鑿，豈有中包一子者。余嘗謂若溪流中多有卵石，容差徧可蕲面磨墨。所謂石子，世因訛爲子石。至有斲様相似而爲之者。於理，必不於大石中心復生卵子也。世之好奇者又以歙州羅文石作子石。硯文本直，兩頭取銳則紋脫短，至左右頰自然成漩紋。便謂之是眞子石。可笑。

綠石帶黃色亦爲硯。多以爲器。材甚美而得墨快。少光彩。已上硯平生約見五七百枚。十千已上無估。

There are four kinds of rock, viz., *hsia-yen* (stone cut from the lower part of the mountain), *shang-yen* (stone cut from the higher parts), *pan-pien-yen* (stone cut from the middle part), and *hou-li-yen* (stones from the Hou-li mountain). I was once in Tuan-chou, that is why I know all details about it.

The *hsia-yen* is the best.[2] When a cave has been hewn deep in the rock, it appears that the stone there is covered with water through all the four seasons. Those who offered ink-stones (from this kind of rock) as tribute during the Chih-p'ing period (1064-1067) had to take away the water for more than one month before they could get at this rock. Generally the stone is fine-grained, and when knocked it has a very clear sound. Its so-called Blackbird-eyes[3] are round and have a blue periphery, being very brilliant. The very soft stones are like clay, they have no sound, and they do not grip the ink. Those that have a clear sound seem to be very damp, they grip the ink and produce quickly, without becoming warm or giving rise to bubbles. After a very long time, however, they will absorb a little, but then they get a beautiful shine, like oil. There are also some that never tire. If one rubs the Fang-ch'êng and Wên-chou stones (*v. supra*) ten times, and these stones thirty times, the result will be about the same. Because these *hsia-yen* stones are hacked from so deep down in the rock, the money spent on the workmen is more than the value of the stone, so that even if one makes the greatest of efforts one cannot buy them, and in later years there has been none. I have heard that before the reign of the Emperor Jên-tsung (1023-1063) many of these stones were offered to the officials of the Board of History; in later years only *shang-yen* stones were offered.

The *shang-yen* stones are hacked from the upper part of the rock.[4] This stone is naturally dry, and it has a deep purple colour. The

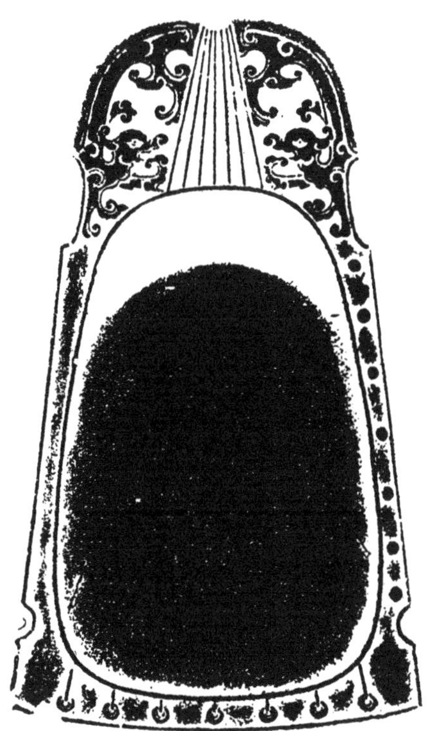

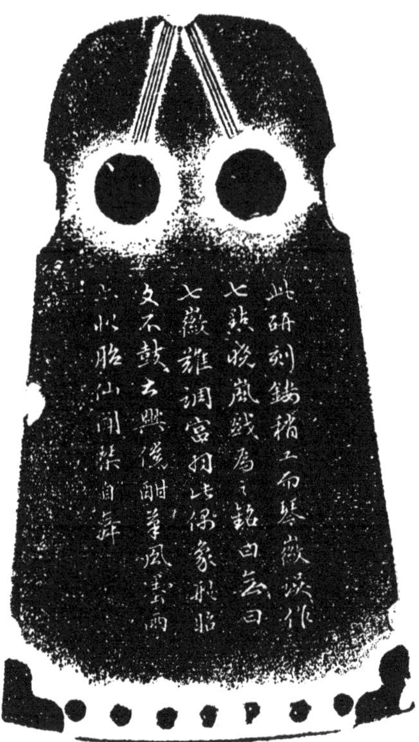

Ink-stone shaped like a Lute, *Ch'in-yang-yen* 琴樣硯
(Collection of Chi Yün)

This ink-stone is carved to represent the ancient seven-stringed lute, *ku-ch'in* 古琴. Both ends of the strings are shown, but in the middle the place where the ink should be rubbed, is carved out. On the right side seven studs are visible. The correct number would be thirteen; the inscription on the reverse refers to this anomaly.

Inscription: "This inkslab has been carved with much care; but the studs are wrongly made to number seven. Therefore I, jestingly, made an inscription for it which says: Do not say that a lute with seven studs can hardly be tuned. This shape occasionally occurs, though it is not played by Chao Wên (a famous lute-player, mentioned in Chuang-tzû, chapter *Hsiao-yao* 逍遙). If the writing succeeds beautifully, then the brush-work will be like wind and rain, and it shall be as if the cranes, hearing the sounds of the lute, start dancing on their own accord."

Note: Since olden times the crane, and especially the dark crane *hsüan-ho* 玄鶴 has been associated with *ch'in* music. Its graceful movements are compared with the finger technique of the *ch'in* player. Chi Yün means to say that whereas a lute designed in the shape indicated by the inkslab could not produce music, an inkslab so shaped can produce ink, and when used by an artist in writing columns of elegant characters, the rhythm of his calligraphy shall also evoke the grace of a dancing crane.

grain is coarse, its nature hard. The spots are yellow and roundish. They have a pale cerulean colour. Deep from the rock occasionally one can get damp ones, but their spots can never be compared to those of the *hsia-yen* stones. Some produce ink easily, others repel the ink. As to the stones which take up ink, the first fortnight one uses them they will produce ink quickly ; this is because of the fine grains of sand of which the surface of the stone is composed. After a fortnight, however, these small grains are ground off, and the stone becomes brilliant. If one wants to apply the inkstick to it, one should first make the surface rough again (by rubbing it) with a soft stone, and then the stone is as before. Those which repel ink will do so even if newly made. If one knocks stones of this kind, they all emit a hard sound, and a sustained echo.

The *pan-pien-yen* is found halfway up the mountain.[5] Its grain is just like that of the *shang-yen*, but the colour is more purplish, nearly black. These stones have many flaws, and the 'eyes' are oblong in shape, like eggs. Among these 'eyes' there are 'blind' ones, with a white spot in the middle. The 'dead eyes' are those that are made indistinct by black spots. The 'thinly filmed' eyes are sometimes cerulean, sometimes black. They are found dispersed among the other 'eyes.' Some are so dark as not to merit the name of 'eyes.' These, however, have oval-shaped spots, which in the cerulean field form a pattern like the grain of pine-wood. The very coarse ones will wear off the hairs of the brush, while the very fine ones will easily tire.

The *hou-li-shih*[6] is used by the local people for making bowls, seals, presses for paper, and toys for children. These stones contain much sand ; they have no spots, and only a few flaws. Among them there are some that are extremely fine and soft. In producing ink they do not easily tire. When knocked this stone has no sound. The local people do not esteem these stones : yet there are indeed some that are superior to *pan-pien* and *shang-yen* stones, but one cannot always obtain them.

Further I have everywhere made enquiries from the stone workers who tell me that (the so-called) 'child-stones' have never existed.[7] These stones are simply the core of the rock. How could one, when boring a big flat rock-plate, find enfolded therein a child? I have always been of the opinion that in rivulets and streams there are many stones shaped like eggs, and of which one side is a little flattened; here one may chisel a face, on which one can rub ink. This is called a 'stone-child,' but people wrongly call it 'child-stone,' while some have even been brought to improve artificially upon this likeness. Their origin, however, is perfectly reasonable: it certainly does not happen that in the heart of a big stone an egg is produced. Those among people to-day who love strange things also make 'child-stones' from stones with criss-cross markings from Hsi-chou. The markings of this stone are as a rule straight. If, however, the stone narrows (runs to a point) at its two ends, the markings are choppy. They verge by natural transitions into whorls on the right and left 'cheeks' of the broadest part of the stone. People call this stone the 'real child-stone.' It is ridiculous!

One can also make inkslabs from a green stone with a streak of yellow in it. Often they make implements from this stone. It is very beautiful material, and one can get ink from it quickly. These stones have a little shine on them. Of the above-mentioned stones I have seen so far about five or seven hundred pieces. The price is at least 10,000 cash.

Annotations. [1] At Tuan-chou, Kao-yao-hsien 高要縣, Kwangtung province, the most famous material for ink-stones is found.—[2] On the slopes of the mountains there are several quarries where, since ancient times, stones have been hewed for making inkslabs. Most famous is the so-called *lao-k'ang* 老坑, "old quarry," which penetrates deep into the rock. This quarry is subdivided into several caves, some of which are permanently under water; therefore the stones from this quarry are also called *shui-yen* 水巖, 'water-stone.' A detailed plan of this quarry, with the special names of all the caves, is to be found in the *Tuan-hsi-yen-shih* and the *Pao-yen-t'ang-yen-pien* mentioned above (*v.* page 20). The so-called *hsia-yen* stones were hacked from this quarry. Stones cut from the layer that was perpetually submerged were valued most. Ink-stones made from stone of this quarry were offered as tribute. Every time the stones had been hewn out the entrance to the cave was closed and sealed, so that no robbers could steal the precious material. The oldest historical reference to stones from Tuan-chou offered as tribute seems to be the statement in the *Sung-shih* 宋史 (太宗紀, ch. 5, page 8 verso), under the year 991 (淳化二年):

"In the fourth month of summer tribute from Tuan-chou consisting of ink-stones was stopped" (夏四月庚午罷端州貢硯).—[3] These eyes or spots in the stone enhance the value of an inkslab considerably. They seem to be mostly fossilized vegetable remains, such as stalks of plants. Connoisseurs value most highly the so-called 'blackbird-eyes,' *ch'ü-yü-yen* 鸜鵒眼; their size is said to vary from that of a *wu-chu* 五銖 coin to a mustard-seed. If they are brilliant, they are called 'living' (*huo* 活); if dull, they are called 'dead' (*ssû* 死). Between these two lie the 'filmed ones,' *i* 翳. If their shape is oblong, they are called 'tears' (*lei* 淚).—[4] Higher up the mountain there were three caves, where the *shang-yen* stone was found.—[5] The *pan-pien-yen* are found in caves more to the east of the "old quarry."—[6] *Hou li* (*shan*) is also written: 後瀝 and 後歷. This mountain lies ten miles to the north, and is also famous for its stones.—[7] On the *tzû-shih* 子石 (variants 仔石 and 紫石) the authorities differ. I have seen some good specimens of this stone. As to its appearance I would say—and I hope that connoisseurs will not call me irreverent!—that it may be compared with a bun: it is round and thick, rather smooth, and without sharp edges. The old idea seems to have been that other stones gave birth to these stones, and that consequently they may be found in the core of a big stone, as it were, in its womb. Some sources call these child-stones the very best of the Tuan-chou variety, while others contend that for the most part they do not produce ink well, and are important only as curiosities. Be this as it may, child-stones are highly valued by connoisseurs. Even to-day they fetch high prices: in Tōkyō early in this year (1936) I was present at an auction of ink-stones, and saw there a *tzû-shih* sold for Yen 600!

VII.—Stones from Wu-yüan, for making Hsi Inkslabs [1]

歙硯婺源石。歙州有硯圖石峒最多種，而赤紫石多瑕。土[a]人以綫，脈，隔，爲三種病。今人以細羅紋無星爲上。少時見一硯於士人趙光弢家。其様上狹四寸許，下闊六寸許。如二十幅紙厚，色綠如公裳，而點如紫金斑。斑匀布無羅紋。點中無竅。自後不復覩與此等者。又士人周昌諤[b]處見一小圓硯。青羅紋一星紫金如鵝眼錢。此二硯最奇。

大抵發墨不乏。獨以色如常之石，而以奇怪爲品高，亦有赤紫色石，無文理，少瑕。光澤如棗木。士人以爲香爐之類。亦斲爲硯。與墨鬭而不相入。經日使滑不可研矣。又嘗[c]士人家見一金絲羅

a. *S.F.* reads: 士, "scholars," which may also be right.

b. *C.F.C.W* gives 鍔.

c. *H.C.T.Y* reads: 于.

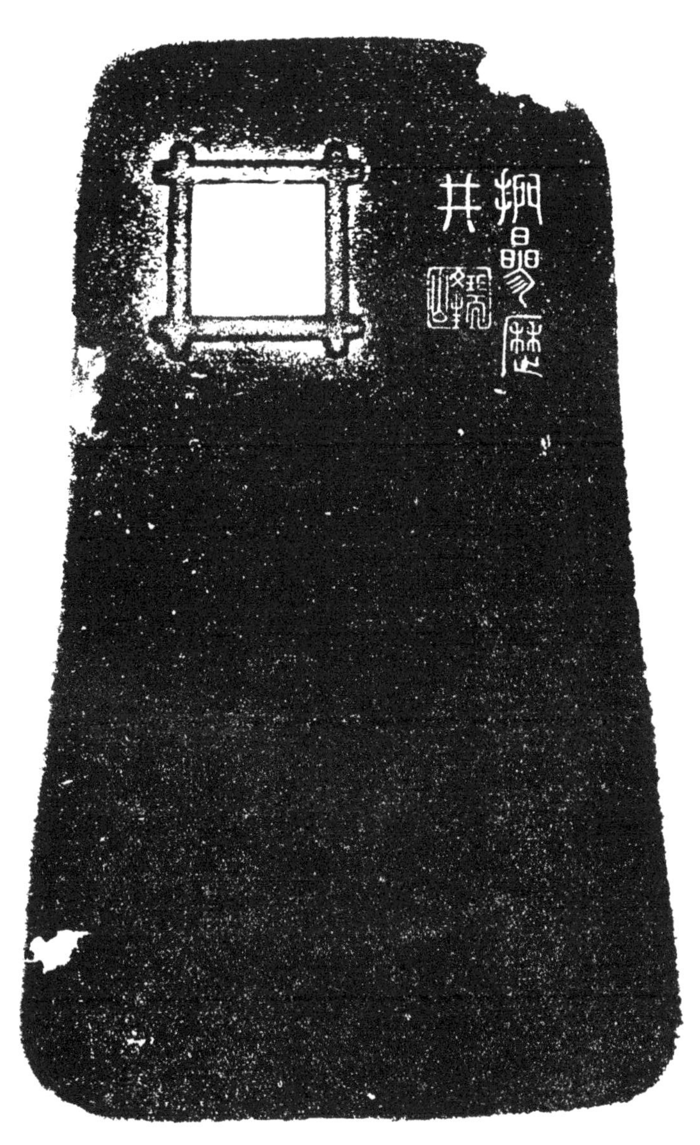

INK-STONE WITH A WELL MOTIF, *Ching-t'ien-yen* 井田硯
(Collection of Chi Yün)

(cf. page 62*n*.)

紋硯。其紋半金半墨，光彩與常異。

此外粗羅紋，刷絲羅紋爲次第。約見千餘枚矣。但以色與瓦磚等，品故不能高。今但曾官歙者必收百餘枚[a]。士人以爲生終日成一硯。少有病，不直數十金。幸完，仍好直。五七千已上無估。

In Hsi-chou there exists a great variety of quarries, where the stone shows an inkslab design.[2] The red and purple stones have many flaws. The local people discern three kinds of shortcomings, viz.: streaks, veins and partitions. Present people consider the stones with a "fine tissue-pattern"[3] and without stars the best. In my youth I saw one ink-stone in the house of the literatus Chao Kuang-pi[4]; its dimensions were over four inches at the top, and more than six at the base. It was as thin as twenty sheets of paper,[5] its colour was green, like princely garments, and it was sprinkled with purple and gold spots. The spots were evenly spread, without forming a pattern. In the spots there were no holes. Never since have I seen a stone like it. Further, I saw in the house of the literatus Chou Ch'ang-ou[6] a small round ink-stone. On a "cerulean tissue-pattern" there showed a purplish golden spot like a star, as big as a Goose-eye coin.[7] These two ink-stones were the most wonderful I have seen.

Generally speaking (the *Hsi-lo-wên* stones) do not tire in producing ink. Because their colour is like that of ordinary stones, however, for those who consider strangeness as a superior quality there are also stones of a red and purple colour, without any markings, and but few flaws. They are glossy like date-wood. The local people use them for making things like incense-burners. Also they cut them into the shape of inkslabs. They repel the ink, so that, during the rubbing, the stone is not mixed with the ink. In course of time they grow slippery, and then can no longer be rubbed. Also I saw once in the house of a scholar an inkslab with a pattern like gold threads. The design was half gold and half black, and the stone had an extraordinary shine.

After these (i.e., the *hsi-lo-wên* stone) come the 'coarse tissue-pattern' and 'brushed-thread tissue-pattern'[8] stones. Altogether I have seen of these a thousand or so pieces. But because their colour is just like that of ordinary bricks, they cannot be esteemed highly. At present the officials who served in Hsi-chou alone must have collected

---

a. *H. C. T. Y* reads: 久, an evident misprint.

more than a hundred pieces. The local people find their livelihood in the making of inkslabs, and in a whole day they make only one. If a stone has only a small fault, it is not worth ever a few tens of copper-pieces; but if an inkslab is happily finished, the price is high, at least from five to seven thousand cash.

Annotations. [1] Hsi-hsien 歙縣, Anhui province. During the T'ang dynasty these stones from Hsi-chou were very popular. According to tradition this stone was discovered in the K'ai-yüan 開元 period (713-741) by a certain Yeh 葉, who, while hunting, penetrated far into the mountains, where his eye suddenly was struck by the beauty of this kind of stone [cf. *Hsi-chou-yen-pu*, mentioned on page 18]. These stones became so well known that at Hsi-chou a special 'ink-stone official,' *yen-wu-kuan* 硯務官, was stationed. At the beginning of the Sung dynasty, however, these quarries were already exhausted. According to another source, a certain Ch'ien Hsien-chih 錢仙芝 during the Ching-yu 景祐 period (1034-1037) discovered at Hsi-chou the old spot where the T'ang painter Li Hou-chu 李後主 (i.e. Li Yü 李煜, 937-978) had found his famous inkslab; but a river flowed through the quarry, so that he could not get at the stones. Then he dammed up the river, and changed its course, and in its bed he found some marvellous stones [cf. *Hsi-yen-shuo* mentioned on page 19]. —[2] The *Pien-hsi-shih-shuo* 辨歙石說 (no date; also incorporated in the *Pai-ch'uan-hsüeh-hai*) enumerates not less than 27 different patterns, each with its special technical name.—[3] *Hsi-lo-wên* stones are described as having an extremely fine criss-cross pattern, like the threads in *crêpe*.—[4] Unidentified.—[5] The Hsi stones were famous for their thinness.—[6] Unidentified.—[7] *O-yen-ch'ien*, a very small coin, which was said to remain floating when placed on water.—[8] These appellations explain themselves.

VIII.—Ink-stones of Mi stone, from Tung-yüan-chün [1]

通遠軍瀃石硯。石理澁可礪刃。綠色如朝衣。深者亦可愛。又[a]則水波紋,間有黑小點,士人謂之湔墨點。有緊甚奇妙而硬者,與墨鬬,而慢甚者滲墨無光。其中者甚佳。在洮河綠石上。自朝廷開熙,河始為中國有。亦有赤紫石,色斑。為硯發墨過於綠者而不勻淨。又有黑者,戎人以礪刀,而鐵色光肥,亦可作硯,而堅不發墨。

The grain of this stone is so hard, that one may sharpen swords on it. Its colour is green, like court-garments, whilst those which have

a. *H. C. T. Y.* reads 久, which seems a misprint.

a deeper colour are lovely too. Also there are some that have a pattern just like waves, sprinkled with small black spots, which the local people call ink-blots. If these spots are dense the stone is really marvellous. But the hard stones repel the ink, while the very soft ones absorb it, so that it does not shine. The middle sort, however, is very beautiful; it surpasses the green stones from the T'ao river. Since during the present dynasty Hsi-chou[2] was explored, this river belongs to China. Also there are red and purple stones, of variegated colours. If one makes ink-stones from them, in producing ink they are better than the green ones, but not so pure. There are also black ones, which are used by the soldiers to sharpen their swords on, by which their colour becomes just like iron, shining and greasy. Also from these stones inkslabs can be made, but they are hard, so that they do not produce ink.

Annotation. [1] At present Lung-hsi-hsien 隴西縣, in Kansu Province. I do not understand the meaning of *Mi* here. Probably it is the name of a rivulet. *K'ang-hsi-tzŭ-tien*, s.v. quoting this passage, simply says that it is the name of a stone from which inkslabs can be made.—[2] At present Lin-t'ao-hsien, in Kansu province.

IX.—Hui-shêng-kung[1] Ink-stones in the Western Capital[2]

西都會聖宮硯。會聖宮石在溪澗中。色紫，理如虢石差硬。發墨不乏。扣之無聲。

The *Hui-shêng-kung* stones are to be found in mountain streams and rivulets. Their colour is purple, their grain is like the *Kuo* stone,[3] but a little harder. In producing ink these stones do not tire; when knocked they emit no sound.

Annotations. [1] *Hui-shêng-kung*, a temple built in 1078; cf. *Ch'ien-ch'üeh-chü-lei-shu* (潛確居類書, publ. 1630 by Ch'ên Yên-hsi 陳仁錫), ch. 43, p. 34.—[2] Hsi-tu, i.e. Lo-yang 洛陽, Lo-yang-hsien, Honan province.—[3] Cf. ch. XXI.

X.—Cerulean Stones from Ch'ing-chou[1]

青州青石。色類歙，理皆不及。發墨不乏。有瓦礫之象。

Their colour is the same as that of the Hsi stones,[2] but they are inferior in grain. In producing ink they do not tire. They resemble tiles.

Annotations. [1] At present I-tu 益都, in Shantung province.—[2] Cf. chapter VII.

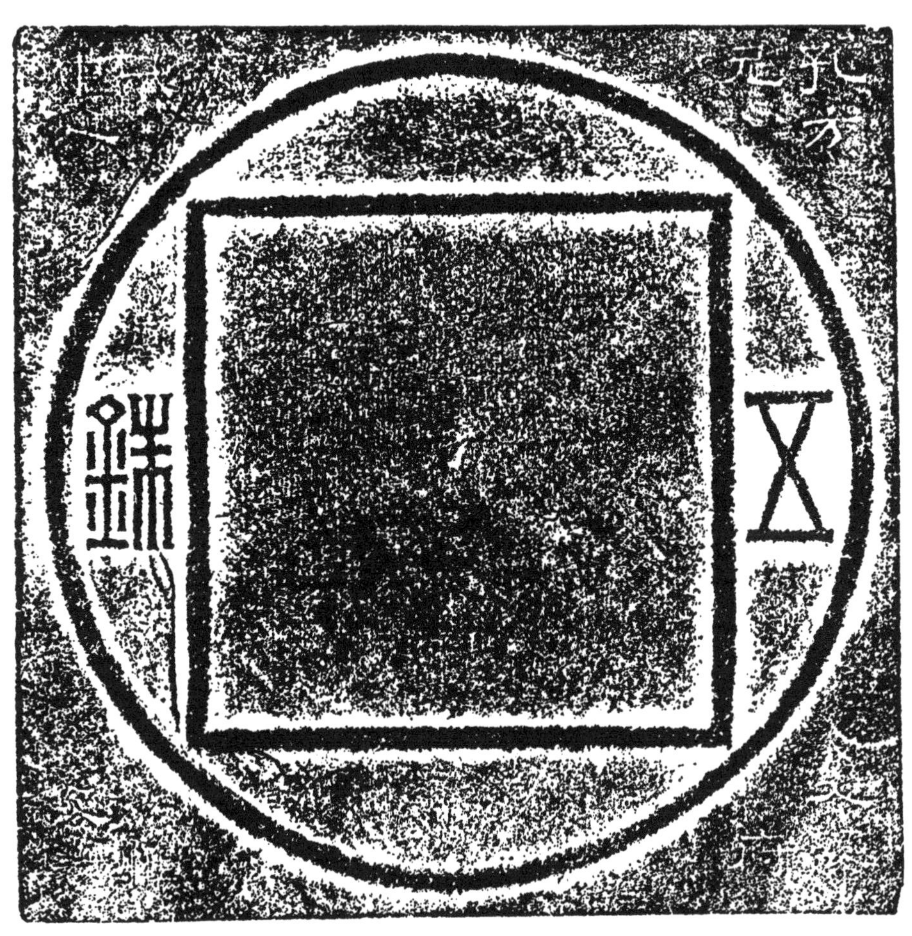

Ink-stone with a Wu-chu Coin Design
(Collection of Chi Yün)

XI.—Stones from Li-t'ing [1] near Ch'êng-chou [2]

成州栗亭石。色青，有銅點大如指。理慢。發墨不乏。亦有瓦礫之象。

Their colour is cerulean, with copper-coloured spots as large as a finger-top. Their grain is sluggish. In producing ink they do not tire. These stones also resemble tiles.

Annotations. [1] Fifteen miles south of Ch'êng-hsien.—[2] Ch'êng-hsien 成縣, in Kansu province.

XII.—Ku-shan [1] Inkslabs from T'an-chou [2]

潭州谷山硯。色淡青，有紋如亂絲。理慢。扣之無聲。得墨快。發墨有光。

They have a flat cerulean colour, and the markings resemble tangled silk threads. Their grain is soft. When knocked, they have no sound. One can quickly get ink from them. While producing ink they will grow brilliant.

Annotation. [1] Ku-shan, also called Yün-mu-shan 雲母山, lies near Ch'ang-sha 長沙.—[2] Ch'ang-sha-hsien, Hunan province.

XIII.—Ink-stones of Chestnut-coloured Jade, at Ch'êng-chou [1]

成州栗玉硯。理堅，色如栗。不甚著墨。爲器甚佳。

Their grain is hard, their colour is like that of a chestnut. They do not take up ink easily. As an implement they are very beautiful.

Annotation. [1] Probably Fêng-ch'uan-hsien 封川縣, in Kwantung province.

XIV.—Green Inkslabs from Kuei-chou [1]

歸州綠石硯。理有風濤之象。紋頭緊慢不等，治難平。得墨快。滲墨無光彩。色綠可愛，如貢。色澹如水蒼玉。

Their grain is like waves stirred by the wind The salient parts of the pattern are not of equal hardness, so that it is difficult to make the stone even. One will quickly obtain ink from them. As they absorb the ink, they do not become brilliant. They have a lovely green colour, with a shining appearance. The colour is pale like *shui-ts'ang* jade.[2]

Annotations. [1] In Hupeh province, Tzû-kuei-hsien 秭歸縣. According to a modern scientific description of the geological conditions in W. Hupeh [C. Y. Hsieh and Y. T. Chao, *Geology of I-chang, Hsing-shan Tzû-kuei and Pa-tung districts*, in "Bulletin of the Geological Survey of China," No. 7, Dec. 1925], the soil near Tzû-kuei consists of green sandstones and purple shales. Evidently Mi Fu means here the green sandstone.—[2] I have not been able to find an explanation of this special kind of jade.

XV.—Inkslabs of Brilliant Black Stone, at Kuei-chou[1]

夔州黟石硯。色黑[a]，理乾。間有墨點，如墨玉光。發墨不乏。

Their colour is black, their grain is dry. They have black spots, resplendent like jet. In producing ink they do not tire.

Annotation. [1] Fêng-chieh-hsien 奉節縣, Ssûch'uan province.

XVI.—Inkslabs from Cerulean Stone, from the Lu Mountain[1]

廬山青石硯。大略與潭州谷山同。

Generally speaking these stones are the same as the Ku-shan stones[2] from T'an-chou.

Annotations. [1] A mountain in Kiangsi province, south of Chiu-chiang-hsien 九江縣.—[2] Cf. chapter XII.

XVII.—Inkslabs of Brownish Stone, at Su-chou[1]

蘇州褐黃石硯。理粗。發墨不滲。類夔石。土人刻成硯，以草一束，燒過爲慢灰火煨之，色遂變紫。用之與不煨者一同。亦不燥。乃知天性非水火所移。

Their grain is coarse. They produce ink without absorbing. They are of the same sort as the Kuei-chou stones.[2] The local people, after they have cut them into the shape of an ink-stone, wrap grass around them, and when this is burnt up, roast them slowly in warm ashes, and then the colour changes into purple. For use, however, they are just the same as the unburnt ones, being not even parched. From which one can see that the original nature can be changed neither by fire nor water.

Annotations. [1] In Kiangsi province—[2] Cf. chapter XV.

XVIII.—An-tan Stones from the Chien River[1]

建溪黯澹石。理如牛角。扣之聲堅清。磨久不得墨，縱得色變如灰。作器甚佳。

---

a. *C. F. C. W* reads 墨, an evident misprint.

Their grain is like that of a cow's horn. When knocked the sound is hard and clear. When they have been rubbed long, one cannot get ink from them any more; or, if one succeeds in getting it, the colour changes and becomes like ash. However, very nice implements can be made from this stone.

Annotation. [1] The Chien-hsi is the northern source of the Min-chiang 閩江 in Fukien province.

XIX.—Ink-stones of Earthenware

陶硯。相州土人自製陶硯，在銅雀上。以熟絹二重淘泥澄之。取極細者燔爲硯。有色綠如春波者。或以黑白填爲水紋。其理細滑，著墨不費筆。但微滲。

The local people of Hsiang-chou [1] themselves make ink-stones of earthenware, which are superior to those of the T'ung-ch'iao terrace. [2] They purify the clay by passing it through a double sieve of seasoned silk. Taking the finest clay they bake inkslabs from it. Among them there are some that have a green colour, just like waves in spring. Some have black and white spots, forming a water-pattern. Their grain is fine and slippery, so that they produce ink, without grinding off the brush; but they absorb a little.

Annotations. [1] An-yang-hsien 安陽縣, Honan province.—[2] This is one of the three pagodas built by Ts'ao Ts'ao 曹操, the famous general of the San-kuo 三國 period. The tiles on the roofs are reputed to make excellent ink-stones: it is said that the rain that falls on them never dries up, so that the stone will remain moist forever. Su I-chien (*op. cit.*, ch. 2, par. 2) says that these tiles derive their exceptional qualities from the fact that they were prepared with walnut-oil. Su I-chien also mentions the fact that the people of Hsiang-chou counterfeited these tile inkslabs.

XX.—Inkslabs shaped like the Character Lü

呂硯。澤州有呂道人陶硯。以別色泥於其首純作呂字內外透。後人效之，有縫不透也。其理堅。重與凡石等。以瀝[a]青火油之。堅響，滲入三分許。磨墨不乏。其理與方[b]城石等。

In Tsê-chou [1] there is a clay ink-stone of the Taoist Lü Tung-pin. [2] By using differently coloured clay on the rims of the upper part,

a. All texts have 歷, which obviously stands for 瀝.

b. *C. F. C. W.* and *F. Y. S.* mistake this for 万, and read 萬.

one gets the character 呂 *lü*, which goes right through the stone. People of later times tried to imitate it, but then the character *lü* is only, as it were, sewn on, and does not penetrate into the stone. Its grain is hard. Its weight is about the same as that of other inkslabs. It is prepared with resin-oil. It has a hard sound, and it absorbs for about three *fên*. Rubbed with ink it does not tire. Its grain is the same as that of the Fang-ch'êng stone.[3]

Annotations. [1] Chin-ch'êng-hsien 晉城縣, Shansi province.—[2] A recluse of the T'ang dynasty, later canonized as one of the Eight Immortals, *Pa-hsien* 八仙.—[3] Cf. chapter IV.

XXI.—Inkslabs from Tzû-chou [1]

淄州硯。淄石理滑。易乏。在建石之次。

The stones from Tzû-chou have a slippery grain. They soon tire. They come next to the stones of the Chien river.[2]

Annotations. [1] Tzû-ch'uan-hsien 淄川縣, Shantung province.—[2] Cf. chapter XVIII.

XXII.—Inkslabs from Korea

高麗硯。理密，堅有聲。發墨。色青間白。有金星，隨橫文密成列。用久乏。

Their grain is compact, and they have a hard sound. They produce ink (easily). Their colour is cerulean, alternating with white. They have golden stars, which are arranged crosswise so as to form rows. After long use they become tired.

XXIII.—Yün-yü stones, Hung-ssû stones and Ch'ing stones from Ch'ing-chou

青州蘊玉石，紅絲石，青石。理密，聲堅清。色清，黑白點如彈。不著墨。墨無光。好事者但置爲一器可。紅絲石作器甚[a]佳。大抵色白而紋紅者慢發墨。亦漬墨不可洗。必磨治之。紋理斑石。赤者不漬墨。發墨有光而紋大不入看。慢者經喝，則色損。凍則裂。乾則不可磨，墨浸，經日方可用。一用又可滌。非品之善。青石有粗紋如羅。近歙。亦著墨不發。

a. The original text has the character 罙, which could be an abbreviation of 深. *S F.* only keeps this character; the other texts change it into 甚, which seems the better reading.

The grain (of Yün-yü stones) is compact, their sound is hard and clear. Their colour is cerulean, with black and white spots like balls. They do not grip the ink, and the ink does not shine; they are good for amateurs who only attach value to things as curios. From Hung-ssû stones particularly fine implements can be made. On the whole, those that have a white colour and red markings produce ink slowly. Moreover, if they are soiled with ink, one cannot wash them; they can only be cleansed by polishing. Among the stones with variegated patterns and markings, the red ones are not soiled by the ink. The ink produced will be shining, but the pattern of the stone is ugly. If the 'slow' ones are exposed to heat, their colour will be spoiled. When it freezes, they crack. When dry, they should not be rubbed, for then the ink will be absorbed by the stone, and they can be used only after many days. Each time after they have been used one should clean them, which proves that this is not a good sort of stone. The Ch'ing stones have a harsh pattern, just like a net. They resemble the Hsi stones. They grip the ink, but they do not produce so easily.

XXIV.—Stones from Kuo-chou [1]

虢州石。理細如泥。色紫可愛。發墨不滲。久之石漸損凹[a]。硬墨磨之則有泥香。

Their grain is fine like clay. They have a lovely purple colour. They produce ink without absorbing. In the course of time the stone will gradually be hollowed out. If one rubs the stone with a hard cake of ink, there will be a smell of clay.

Annotation. [1] South-west of Ling-pao-hsien 靈寶縣, Honan province.

XXV.—Crystal inkslabs from Hsin-chou [1]

信州水晶硯，於他硯磨墨，汁傾入用。

One should rub the ink on another inkstone, and then, having poured the ink over on it, use this stone.

Annotation. [1] Shang-jao-hsien 上饒縣, Kiangsi province.

XXVI.—White Inkslabs from Ts'ai-chou [1]

蔡州白硯，理滑。可爲器，爲朱硯。花蘂石，亦作小朱硯。

a. The original text, and all others read 回, which I take to be a misprint for 凹.

Their grain is slippery. One can make implements from them, and inkslabs for vermilion ink. Of *Hua-jui* stones[2] one can also make small ink-stones for vermilion ink.

Annotations. [1] Ju-nan-hsien 汝南縣, Honan province.—[2] *Hua-jui* stones (flower-petal stones) come from Wên-hsiang-hsien 閺鄉縣, also in Honan province. Their colour is said to resemble tortoise-shell.

XXVII.—On the different qualities of Ink-stones

性品。大抵四方硯發墨久不乏者，石必差軟。叩之聲低而有韻。歲久漸凹。不發墨者石堅。叩之堅[a]響。稍用則如鏡走墨。余所品謂目擊自收經用者。聞雖多不錄以傳。疑古硯無不佳。豈不嘗落。非好事者手用之則尋棄擲之矣，惟久在人間，賢庸並善。是以不乏傳也。

Generally speaking, all inkslabs, irrespective of their place of provenience, will produce ink during a long time, without becoming 'tired,' if the stone is comparatively soft. If one knocks them, they have a low, harmonious sound. After many years they become hollowed out. Of those stones that do not produce ink (easily), the material is hard. When knocked they have a hard sound. After a little use they look like a mirror, and the ink runs (i.e., while rubbing slips away from under the stick of ink). All the stones I have classified here I have seen with my own eyes, and I have collected and used them myself. Those about which I have merely heard, even if it be a great deal, I have not put in my record. I suspect that all old stones were without exception beautiful. This being the case, why have they never been lost? People who were not interested in these things had, it is true, the habit of throwing them away after they had used them. But only because (these same stones) have been a long time among men, worthy men and mediocre men appreciate them alike. And for this reason (the old stones) never cease to circulate.

XXVIII.—On the various kinds of Ink-stones

樣品。晉硯見於晉顧愷之畫者，有於天生疊石上刊人面者。有十蹄，圓銅硯中如鏨者，余嘗以紫石作之。有上圓下方，於圓純上刊兩竅置筆者。有如鳳字兩足者，獨此甚多，所謂鳳凰池也。

a. *H. C. T. Y* and *C. F. C. W.* read 聲, which must be a misprint.

蓋以上並晉製見於晉人圖畫。世俗呼爲風字,蓋不原兩足之製,謂之鳳足。至今端州石工以兩眼相對於足傍者,謂之鳳足。鳳之義取五色英文,燦然成章也。今人有收得右軍硯。其製與晉圖畫同。頭狹四寸許,下闊六寸許,頂兩純皆綽慢,下不勒成痕。外如內之製。足狹長,色紫,類溫岩。中凹成臼。又有收得智永硯。頭微圓。又類箕象,中亦成臼矣。又有人收古銅硯,一龜銜一硯,如蓮葉,兩足。龜腹圓,墨水不可出。以筆頭就之則出。

又參政蘇文簡家,收唐畫唐太宗長孫后納諫圖。宮人於瑪瑙盤中托一圓頭鳳池[a]硯,似晉製。頭純直,微凸,如書鳳字。左右純斜[b]刊。下不勒痕摺,向頂亦然,不滯墨。其外隨內,勢簡易。

其後至隋唐,工稍巧。頭圓,身微瘦。下闊而足或圓爲柱。已不逮古。

至本朝變成穹高,腰瘦,刃闊,如[c]鉞斧之狀。仁廟已前硯多作此製,後差少。資政殿學士蒲傳正收真宗所用硯,與仁廟賜駙馬都尉李公炤鳳池硯形製一同。至今尙方多此製。國初已來,公卿家往往有之。仁宗已前賜史院官硯皆端溪石。純薄,上狹下闊,峻直不出足[d]。中坦夷。猶有鳳池之像。或有四邊刊花,中爲魚爲龜者。凡此形製多端下岩奇品也。

嘉祐末硯樣已如大指粗心甚凸。意求渾厚而氣象益不古。純斗[e],故勒深,滯墨難滌,心凸,故點筆不圓,常如三角簇[f]。蓋古硯皆心凹,後稍正平,未有凸者。始自侍讀學士唐彥猷作紅絲辟雍硯,心高凸至作馬蹄樣,亦心凸至磨墨溜向身出。觀墨色則凸高增浮泛之勢。撥毫則非便也。其晉銅硯雖如鏊然頂殊平,以便撥毫。

今杭州龍華寺收梁傅大夫瓷硯一枚,甚大,磁褐色,心如鏊,環水如辟雍之製。下作浪花擢環近足處,而磨墨處無磁油,然殊著墨,古墨稱螺,亦恐不若近世堅。不然殆不可磨也。

又丹陽人多於古塚得銅硯,三足蹄,有蓋。不鏤花,中陷一片陶。今人往往作硯於其中,翻以爲匣也。唐墓中,間有得如蓮葉,中凹,兩足如鳳池之製,甚薄,足或如棗也。今歙人最多作形製,而[g]士人尤重[h]端樣,以平直斗樣爲貴。得美石無瑕必先作此樣,滯墨甚可惜也。大抵石美無瑕方可施工。璞而厚者,士人多識其

a. *C.F.C.W.* leaves out 池.

b. *S.F.* has 料, obviously a misprint.

c. *H.C.T.Y.*, *C.F.C.W.*, and *F.Y.S.* leave out this 如.

d. *H.C.T.Y* reads 呈.

e. 斗 evidently standing for 陡.

f. 簇 standing for 鏃.

g. *S.F* leaves out 而.

h. *S.F.* here inserts 而.

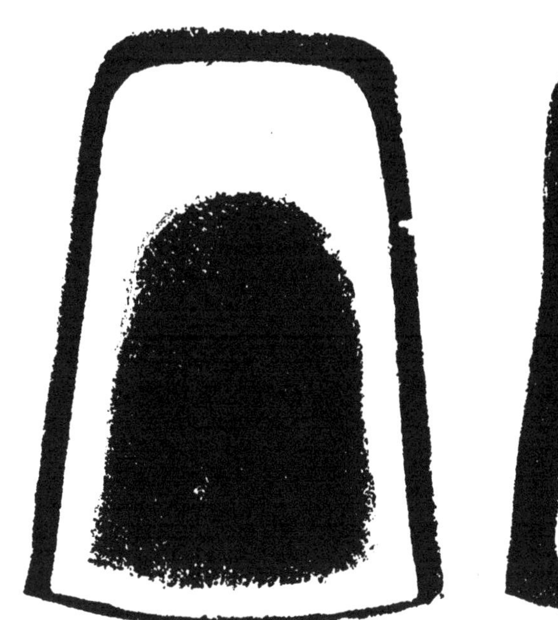

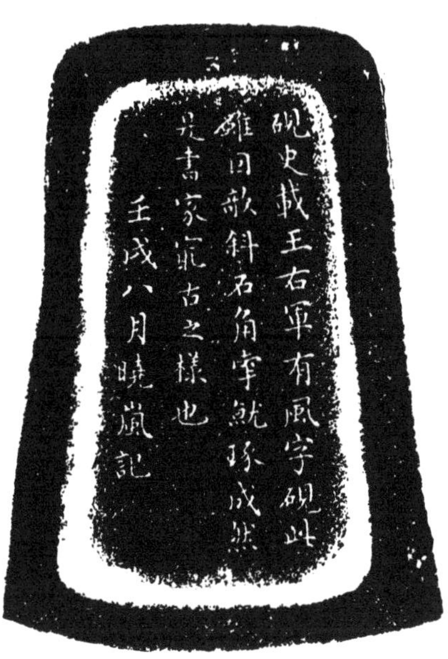

'WIND' CHARACTER INK-STONE, *Fêng-tzû-yen* 風字硯
(Collection of Chi Yün)

INSCRIPTION: "The *Yen-shih* mentions an inkslab of Wang Hsi-chih, having the shape of the character "wind" (cf. chapter XXVIII, page 51). Although this stone is carved slopingly, its corners are rounded off. This is the oldest shape of the ink-stone of calligraphers.

Written by Shao-lan in the year 1802, the 8th month."

澀疾，不復巧製。人或因其渾厚而美之。予嘗惡歙樣。俗者凡刋改十餘硯，纔半指許，便有病見，頓令人減愛。其端，人不斲成，祗持[a]璞，賣者，亦多如是。

陳文惠丞相家收一蜀王衍時皇太子陶硯，連蓋。蓋上有鳳坐一臺，餘雕雜花草，涅之以金泥紅漆。有字曰鳳凰臺。此製方直上狹，筭[b]在硯上。中甚平也。

唐之製見文房四譜，今之製見歙州硯圖。故不重出。此人力所爲也。

吾收一青翠疊石。堅響。三層，傍一嵌磨墨。上出一峯高尺餘。頂復平。嵌岩如亂雲四垂以覆硯。以水澤頂，則隨葉垂珠滴硯心。上有銘識。事[c]見唐莊南傑賦。乃歷代所寶也。

又收一正紫石。四疊。下有坐，有足，巧於瘿盂。足上起一枝細狹，枝上盤兩疊，長七寸餘，闊四寸餘，如靈芝。首銳下闊。天然鳳池之象。中微凹，點水磨墨可書十幅紙。石理在方城之右。此非人力所成。信天下之瓌寶也。

Among the ink-stones of the Chin period that are seen in the pictures of Ku K'ai-chih,[1] there are some made naturally in layers, and on which a human face is carved. There are also round bronze inkslabs, with ten supports; the inside of these is shaped like a pan. I used to make inkslabs shaped like these out of purple stone. Some are round at the top and square at the base; in the rim of the rounded part of the inkslab (i.e. at the top) they carve two holes, to put the brush in (when not in use). Some have two 'feet,' just like the character for phœnix (i.e. its outline 几); this kind is very common, and is called 'Phœnix-pond.' Together with the above-mentioned slabs of Chin make, they may be seen in the pictures of the Chin painters. They are commonly called after the character 'wind' [which also shows the 几 outline; in Mi Fu's opinion, however, the character 'Phœnix' is the correct one, because it refers also to the long feet of this auspicious bird], for people do not realize that the form with two feet is named after the feet of the Phœnix. Up till now the stones from Tuan-chou[2] have been made with the two 'eyes' opposite each other, by the side of the feet, and these slabs are also called 'Phœnix-feet.' But here the

a. Most of the texts have 特; *C. F. C. W* and *M. S. T. S.* change this in 持, which I have adopted here.

b. I take 筭 as standing for 箕, though I cannot say it makes the text much clearer.

c. *H. C. T. Y.* reads 字.

word ' Phœnix ' refers to the bright pattern of five colours [the Phœnix is described as being decked with five colours, just as its voice is composed of the five tones], which is brilliant, to the point of having perfect elegance. At present a certain man has in his collection the inkslab of Wang Hsi-chih.[3] Its construction tallies with the pictures of the Chin period. It is narrow at the top, being a little more than four inches, and broad at the base, being a little more than six inches. The two rims at the top are without any decoration, nor is the lower part carved. Outside and inside it is just the same. Its ' feet ' are thin and long, its colour is purple, just like the Wên-chou stones.[4] Inside it is concave, so as to form a mortar. There is also another person who has in his collection the inkslab of Chih Yung.[5] At the top it is rounded off a little, and it is shaped like a basket, the inside having also the form of a mortar. There is also someone who has in his collection an old bronze inkslab ; it consists of a tortoise, having in its mouth an inkslab, shaped like a lotus-leaf, which is supported by two feet. The belly of the tortoise is convex, so that the ink cannot come out. It only comes out when urged by the tip of the brush.

Further, there is in the house of the Counsellor Su Wên-chien[6] a picture of the T'ang dynasty representing the Empress Ch'ang Sun admonishing the Emperor T'ai-tsung.[7] There, one sees a number of courtiers presenting, on an agate dish, a Phœnix-pond inkslab, rounded off at the top, made like the slabs of the Chin period. The rim at the top is straight, and a little protuberant, just as one writes the character ' Phœnix.' The brims on the right and the left are hewn into slopes ; the lower part shows no ripples or wrinkles, and towards the upper part the slab is just the same (i.e., even), so that the ink can flow freely. The exterior is just like the interior. Its general features are simple.

Afterwards, coming to the Sui and T'ang periods, the workmanship (of the ink-stones) becomes a little more elaborate. At the top they are round, their main body is slim; at the base they are broad, and sometimes their feet are round, serving as struts. But they do not reach the perfection of the old ink-stones.

Arriving at the present dynasty the stones were made larger, their middle remained slim, with a broad sharp side, just like the shape of a halberd or an axe. Before the reign of Jên-tsung (1023-1063) most stones were fashioned in this way; but afterwards stones of this shape become rather rare. The *Tzû-chêng-tien-hsüeh-shih* P'u Tsung mêng [8] added to his collection the inkslab of Chên-tsung (998-1022), which is of the same make as the Phœnix-pond inkslab, given by Jên-tsung to the Imperial son-in-law Li Kung-chao.[9] Up to the present time the craftsmen of the Imperial household for the most part make inkslabs of this design. Since the beginning of this dynasty princes and ministers use these stones more and more. Before the reign of Jên-tsung, however, the inkslabs presented to the officials of the Board of History were all Tuan or Hsi stones. They have thin rims, and are narrow at the top and broad at the base; the sides are quite straight, so that they do not show 'feet.' Their centre is flat. There are also some that have the shape of Phœnix-pond inkslabs. Some are decorated on their four sides with carvings, having in their centre a fish or a tortoise. The stones of this make are mostly wonderful specimens of the *Tuan-hsia-yen* sort.[10]

At the end of the Chia-yu period (1056-1063), the inkslabs were shaped like a thumb, with their centre bulging out. Although simplicity and solidity are intended, these slabs do not show the old shape. As the rims are high, the cavity where the water accumulates is low, so that it is difficult to wash away the dried up ink: and because their centre is bulging, the point of the brush (when applied to the inkslab to moisten it with ink) is not round, but always remains like a three-cornered arrow-head. The old inkslabs all had a concave centre; later on they were a little flattened, but still not bulging. It was only from the time when the *Shih-tu-hsüeh-shih* T'ang Hsün [11] began to make *Pi-yung* inkslabs [12] of Hung-ssû stone [13] that their centre became high and bulging, so as to form the shape of a horse-hoof. Sometimes their centre bulges to such a degree as to make the ink flow away sideways along the body of the slab. With regard to the colour of the ink it will be observed that very bulging slabs tend to make the ink shallow; moreover it is not easy to apply the brush to these slabs. The bronze inkslabs of the Chin period, although they are shaped like a pan, are flattened at the top, in order to make it easy to apply the brush to them.

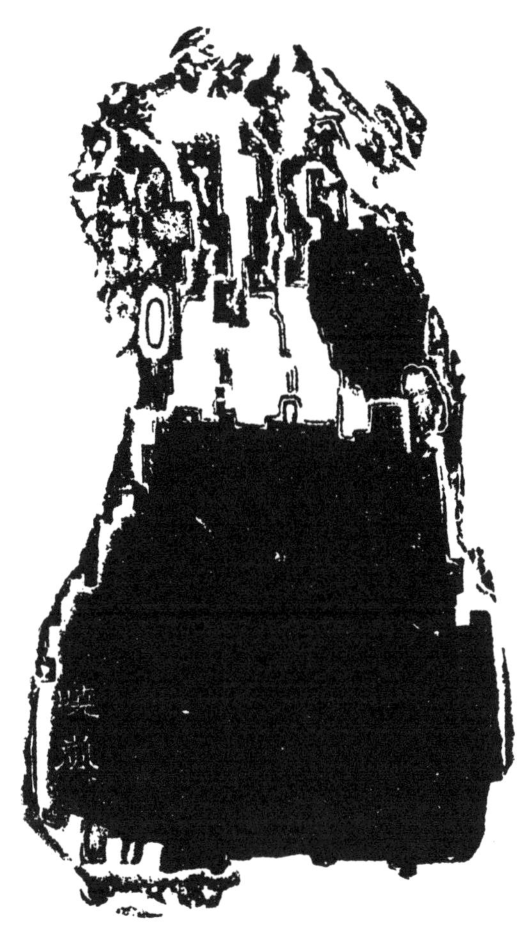

INK-STONE WITH 'PINE-BARK' PATTERN
(Collection of Chi Yün)
The lower left corner shows Chi Yün's signature: Shao-lan

At present in the Lung-hua temple at Hang-chou there is preserved an earthenware inkslab, handed down from high officials of the Liang dynasty (502-557). It is very large, and the material has a brown colour. Its centre is shaped like a pan, and it is surrounded by water, just like the *Pi-yung* model. It is carved with a pattern that resembles foam on waves, and which, near the feet, covers the circumference. The place where the ink is to be rubbed is not glazed, so that it grips the inkstick well. The inksticks of olden times were called 'shell,' [14] but still I surmise they were not so hard as those of later times. If not, (earthenware inkslabs) could hardly be rubbed.

The people of Tan-yang [15] very often find in old tombs bronze inkslabs, with three supports, and a cover. They are not adorned with chase-work. Inside is sunk a cake of clay. The present people more and more place inkslabs in them, or turn them upside down and use them as boxes (for inkslabs). In the graves of the T'ang dynasty one may occasionally find inkslabs shaped like lotus-leaves. Their centre is concave, they have two 'feet,' like the Phœnix-pond inkslabs, and they are very thin. Sometimes the feet are shaped like dates. At present the people of Hsi-chou [16] mostly fashion inkslabs in this way, but the local people value especially the Tuan models. Those that are flat and straight like a bushel are valued most highly. If they get a beautiful stone without flaws, they always first carve it into this shape. Then the ink will coagulate (in the corners), which is a great pity. Generally people work with care only stones that are beautiful and without flaws; if stones are left plain and thick, it is usually because the local people have recognized some hidden faults, and did not care to work them elaborately. People sometimes praise them for their plainness and solidity, but I have always disliked the Hsi models. I have tried to change some ten stones of this unelegant shape by recarving them, but at the depth of half a finger faults appeared, which suddenly made one like them less. The Tuan stones that are not carved into any shape, but just left as they are, and sold in this rough condition, in most cases are the same as these (i.e., when carved they are liable to show hidden faults).

In the house of the Prime Minister Ch'ên Yao-tso [17] there is preserved a clay inkslab that once belonged to Wang Yen [18] of Shu in the days when he was Heir-apparent. It has a cover, and on that cover is a phœnix, sitting on a platform richly decorated with carvings of flowers and plants, gilded and painted with red varnish. The inscription on it reads: 'Phœnix Terrace'; (this platform) has a square shape, narrow at the top, and it is put over the ink-stone like a traverse. Its centre is very flat.

The models of the T'ang period, one may find described in the *Wên-fang-ssû-pu*,[19] while the present models may be seen in the *Hsi-chou-yen-t'u*.[20] Therefore I will not discuss again here these inkslabs, which are all artificially modelled.

I have in my collection a greenish blue stone, made in layers. It has a hard sound. It consists of three layers, and by the side of each is chiselled out a place for rubbing the ink. At the top it rises into a peak of more than a foot high, the summit of which, again, is flat. The stone is carved with confused clouds, descending along the four sides, and covering the inkslab. If one moistens the top with water, then the drops flowing along the leaves will wet the centre of the inkslab. On the top there is an inscription. Consult the poetical description by Chuang Nan-chieh.[21] This stone has been treasured for generations.

I have also in my collection a stone of pure purple colour, consisting of four layers. At the base there is a pedestal, with supports, carved like a bowl with protuberances. On this pedestal rises a thin branch, and this branch supports the two other layers, shaped like dishes, which measure seven odd inches in length and four odd inches in breadth. This stone, in shape, resembles the holy *chih* fungus.[22] The slab is thin at the top and broad at the base, having naturally the shape of a Phœnix-pond slab. In the centre this slab is slightly concave: if one pours out a little water here, and rubs ink, the ink will prove sufficient to cover with characters ten rolls of paper. The grain of this stone is even better than that of the Fang-ch'êng inkslabs.[23] It is not artificially made into this shape. I believe it to be a great treasure of the Empire.

Annotations.—[1] The famous painter of the "Admonitions of the Instructress in the Palace," 4th century A.D.—[2] Cf. chapter VI.—[3] Style: I-shao 逸少; 321-379; the paragon of Chinese calligraphers.—[4] Cf. chapter V.—[5] A famous calligrapher of the Ch'ên 陳 dynasty.—[6] Unidentified.—[7] The incident referred to is probably that on account of the minister Wei Chêng 魏徵; cf. C. P. FitzGerald, *Son of Heaven*, a biography of Li Shih-min, founder of the T'ang Dynasty, Cambridge 1933, p. 158 : " On one occasion the emperor left the counsel in a state of great irritation with Wei Chêng, who had consistently and vigorously opposed him in the discussion. As he entered the apartments of the empress she heard him exclaim : 'I will never be the master as long as that wretch, whom I have raised from the dust, is alive ! ' . . . . . The empress made no further comment, but withdrew to her own room, presently reappearing dressed in her most magnificent robes of ceremony. Shih-min, surprised, asked the reason for this elaborate toilet. The empress replied : 'I have often heard it said, that an enlightened emperor will find a faithful minister, upright and sincere. Your Majesty has just admitted that Wei Chêng is such a one. Is this not a proof that you are an enlightened emperor ? I have robed myself in honour of the fact, to congratulate you.' "—[8] Style : Ch'uan-chêng 傳正, cf. Sung-shih, ch. 328. The Tzû-cheng palace was built by Chên-tsung, as a part of the Lung-t'u-ko 龍圖閣. He specially created the title *Tzû-chêng-tien-hsüeh-shih* for his favourite Wang Ch'in-jo 王欽若, but later this title was also conferred on other persons.—[9] Unidentified.—[10] Cf. chapter VI.—[11] Style : Yen-yu 彥猶, the author of the *Yen-lu* ; *v. supra*, page 14.—[12] Inkslabs made after the model of the Pi-yung-kung 辟雍宮, an old Imperial institute ; the building was situated in the centre of a circular pond. Next to the temple of Confucius at Peking there now exists a Pi-yung-kung, built in 1783 by the emperor Ch'ien-lung. *Pi-yung* inkslabs have a circular form ; in the centre is an elevated round platform, where the ink is rubbed ; the surrounding gully is filled with water.—[13] Cf. chapter XXIII.—[14] I have not been able to find this term elsewhere.—[15] In Hupeh province.—[16] Cf. chapter VII.—[17] 陳堯佐, 963-1044 ; his posthumous name was Wên-hui.—[18] His original name was Tsung-yen 宗衍 ; afterwards he changed it into Wang Yen. He succeeded his father as king of Shu 蜀, and was notorious for his cruelty. Later he was attacked and defeated by Chuang-tsung 莊宗 (923-926) of the later T'ang dynasty.—[19] Cf. *supra*, page 18.—[20] Cf. *supra*, page 18.—[21] A poet of the 9th century A.D. The *fu* mentioned here is to be found in Su I-chien's *Wên-fang-ssû-pu* chapter on ink-stones, section *Tz'û-fu* 辭賦.—[22] The *chih* is a kind of agaric, symbol of longevity.—[23] Cf. chapter IV.

CHAPTER IV

CONCLUSIONS

In composing an essay in the Chinese literary language, a great difficulty one is confronted with is to retain the direct contact of sensation and expression. The reason lies in the particular nature of the Chinese *wên-li* 文理, which in the Sung dynasty had already become entirely separated from the spoken word. The *wên-li* is a highly polished, special idiom, which can successfully be used only by literati who have spent many years in committing to memory the basic texts of Chinese literature, in order to become acquainted with all the myriad stylistic figures and twists of which this excellent vehicle of thought is composed. In trying to express a sensation in this literary idiom, many special expressions and metaphors immediately present themselves to the mind of the composer. And in his mind they are not conceived as isolated expressions, but retain an association with the original context. So, while choosing one of them, the composer is liable to become, often without noticing it, engrossed in the train of thought of the writer of the original text from which the quotation is taken : his own sentiment is thus supplanted by that of the writer quoted. The result may be a highly polished essay, but it will not give the impression of being a specimen of true literary art. Although the style may be impeccable, the reader feels that contact between the real sensation and its expression has been broken, that the inspiration of the composer was too weak to maintain itself against the sentiment that inspired the classical model. Only the real artist can choose his quotations so well that they support his own thoughts, and by a subtle shade of meaning in the context of the original even add poignancy to his own expression. So in old Chinese literature, style and content are intimately correlated, a fact often overlooked by critics of Chinese literature.

The same difficulty of sticking to one's own ideas occurs in relation to the subject matter of a Chinese essay. There is hardly a topic dear to the Chinese literati that has not been treated already by several earlier authors. So here, too, the composer of a new study is liable to become lost in quotations from, and opinions of, other writers in the same field. His own contribution will turn out to be little but the expression of more or less conventionalized opinions of others. The work then becomes a compilation, of which there exist countless specimens in all branches of Chinese literature. As works of reference these books are extremely useful, but they are far from belonging to the higher class of literature.

It seems worth while to view the *Yen-shih* of Mi Fu in the light of these considerations, and to compare it with other essays on ink-stones of the same period. As I have already pointed out in Ch. II, in Mi Fu's time the study of ink-stones was very popular. Mi Fu knew the books of Su I-chien and of T'ang Hsün, and also the *Hsi-chou-yen-pu*. It may be safely assumed that he also knew some of the others, although he does not quote them. Yet from beginning to end his *Yen-shih* is a record of the results of independent investigation, without a single sentence copied from any of the other books. Mi Fu utilizes the material collected by them, but only to test and verify his own observations. In a true scientific spirit he does not let himself be led away by the opinions of others, but firmly sticks to the objects that lie before him. Or, to use his own words: "All the stones I have classified here I have seen with my own eyes, and I have collected and used them myself. Those about which I have merely heard, even if it be a great deal, I have not put in my record" (cf. chapter XXVII).

Putting Mi Fu's treatise side by side with Su I-chien's chapter on ink-stones, we cannot but see how widely their methods in treating this subject differ. Su I-chien's book is moulded after the *I-wên-lei-chü* 藝文類聚 of Ou-yang Hsün 歐陽詢 (style: Hsin-pên 信本, 557-641); to imitate this huge work of literary reference [1] while treating a comparatively limited subject like that of writing-materials is like carving a chicken with a butcher's chopper. He took the standpoint of a registrar of scattered references, dividing the section on ink-stones into four parts: viz.: I. *Hsü-shih* 敘事, "Classified references"; II. *Tsao* 造, "How

[1] Cf. *An annotated bibliography of selected Chinese reference-works*, Harvard-Yenching Institute, 1936, p. 88.

to make ink-stones" ; III. *Tsa-shuo* 雜說, " Miscellaneous Quotations" ; and IV. *Tz'û-fu* 辭賦, " Literary compositions." Part I begins with what according to traditional standards should be the beginning : the ink-stone of the mythical Emperor Huang Ti ! Then follows a motley collection of references, put one after the other, without any logical sequence. Part II contains some remarks about the cutting of ink-stones, and about the baking of earthenware inkslabs, for the greater part extracts from other books. Also some anecdotes on ink-stones are quoted. The contents of Part III are essentially the same as those of Part II, only the narrative element is here more apparent. In Part IV, which forms the bulk of the treatise, a number of purely literary compositions, having some bearing upon ink-stones, are quoted in their entirety. So Su I-chien does not even bother to sift this incoherent mass, nor does he try to arrive at more general and comprehensive observations and put clearly to the reader the problem of the ink-stone. The book is just a collection of jottings, and one is obliged to read it through from beginning to end in order to find what one is looking for.

T'ang Hsün's *Yen-lu* is in many respects exactly the opposite of Su I-chien's book. T'ang Hsün does not follow any fixed plan, nor does he give historical data ; already at the very beginning he takes to a broadly narrative style. While Su I-chien is too much addicted to the piling up of isolated quotations, T'ang Hsün, on the contrary, smoothly incorporates many scraps of useful information in the course of his narrative, making a very readable account, but without succeeding in composing a scientifically justified, surveyable essay.

Ou-yang Hsiu's *Yen-pu* is so brief that we here may leave it out of consideration. Evidently it is not meant to be a finished study. The style, however, is excellent, as befits a scholar of his high standing.

Chu Ch'ang-wên in his remarks on ink-stones follows the old Chinese encyclopedic method of incorporating works of other authors in their entirety. In this treatise the booklet of T'ang Hsün is to be found, and the greater part of Su I-chien's chapter on ink-stones.

When we compare the plan and arrangement of these books with that of Mi Fu's treatise, the scientific and artistic superiority of the latter is evident.

In his introduction Mi Fu defines his attitude with regard to the subject matter: "Let each man have his hobby; if this hobby is rather out of the common, this can certainly be no reason to consider it as inferior." Here appears the individualism of the artist, by nature, opposed to the feelings of the masses. Next he points out that one must not look down upon the subject-matter because of its comparative smallness. To express this idea Mi Fu needs but one phrase, an elaboration of an appropriate quotation from the *Lun-yü*, whereas Su I-chien in his epilogue needs four quotations for expounding the same thought. Though his epilogue is very cleverly written (especially the elaboration of the *ni* 泥 idea is well done), in my opinion Mi Fu's preface through its brilliant terseness stands on a higher literary level.

In the plan of the work the differences between Mi Fu's treatise and those of his predecessors become still more apparent.

After stating his sentimental views Mi Fu proceeds to define his scientific standpoint regarding the subject matter. He immediately grasps the essential point: the all-important criterium for an ink-stone is not its colour, nor its shape and workmanship, but only the degree to which it answers its purpose: the producing of ink. None of his predecessors had arrived at the formulation of this important fact.

Having thus clearly defined the general aspect of the problem, Mi Fu gives, in a series of separate chapters, descriptions of various kinds of ink-stones, classified according to their places of origin. Then he once more returns to more general questions, and discusses first the nature of ink-stones, *Hsing-p'in* 性品 and finally their different shapes, *Yang-p'in* 樣品. The text as published in the *Ch'ün-fang-ch'ing-wan ts'ung shu* (*v. supra* page 15), which professes to be a redaction by Mao Chin, inserts these two concluding chapters directly after the second, *Yung-p'in* 用品. The motive for this alteration is probably that all these three chapters are called *p'in*, "classification," which made the editor of the text think that they belonged together. The *Mei-shu-ts'ung-shu* in the second edition (1928) also adopts this arrangement, without mentioning, however, the *Ch'ün-fang-ch'ing-wan*; it only gives the name of Mi Fu as author, without any indication as to the redaction of the text. In the first edition (1910) the *Mei-shu-ts'ung-shu* reproduces the text as published by Chang Hai-p'êng, in the *ts'ung-shu*: *Hsüeh-chin-tao-yüan* (see page 15).

I do not think this alteration of the sequence of the chapters is a happy one. The chapter *Yung-p'in* is clearly introductory, while *Hsing-p'in* and *Yang-p'in* are essentially retrospective: they are at their right place at the end of the treatise. Besides, all other editions have the same sequence as that of the text of the *Pai-ch'uan-hsüeh-hai*.

While treating the various sorts of ink-stones Mi Fu is concise and to the point. He does not indulge in historical quotations referring to high antiquity: his historical data refer mostly to the T'ang dynasty, which period nearly immediately preceded the Sung dynasty. When he speaks of ink-stones from the Chin period, he relies on archæological data such as paintings of that period, inkslabs found in tombs, and stones which had been transmitted in the families of literati from one generation to another. If a modern sinologue were to compose a history of ink-stones he could not choose a better method.

The style is original and simple, without unnecessary complicated literary allusions. Mi Fu coined many new terms relating to ink-stones, which have been adopted by his successors.

Mi Fu shows himself particularly keen on distinguishing fact from fiction. This is apparent in his frank scepticism with regard to the "child-stones" (ch. VI), and the exceptional qualities ascribed to old inkslabs (ch. XXVII).

Those critical reflections, however, do not dull his genuine enthusiasm for his subject. Therefore the last phrase, in which he expresses his admiration for a special stone, exclaiming: "It is a great treasure of the empire," is a worthy conclusion to his brief essay.

In this connection I may be allowed to translate here a poem[1] that Mi Fu devoted to his ink-stone:

By the well, with its richly carved borders,
    A pond is born, lonely and cool.
The paper window, where I am reading,
    Shows the glimmering flight of the fireflies.

---

[1] Cf. *Pao-chin-ying-kuang-chi*, ch. 5: 金井寒生一水池。讀書窗紙照螢飛。悲歡窮泰尋常共。擲破還須匣取歸. In my translation I have not been able to do justice to this exquisite poem, rich in subtle suggestions. The first line refers to the ink-stone, to the cavity on top, filled with pure water, and generally decorated with carvings. 金井 lit. "golden well" stands for "elegance." The

Sorrow and mirth, poverty and opulence,
    We have shared together, you and I.
And when we are cast away and broken,
    Still a coffin awaits the Return—
                                    Yours and mine.

Finally, if I may sum up the impressions one obtains from a perusal of Mi Fu's *Yen-shih*, comparing it with other treatises on the same subject, I would say that here Mi Fu presents himself as a critical spirit, gifted with a sharp sense of discrimination, and endowed with unusual logical capacity. And it is because this perspicacity is combined with artistic creative powers of the highest order that Mi Fu must, I think, be considered as one of the most important art-critics in Chinese history.

---

pond is the place where the ink is rubbed, after having been moistened with water from the " well " on top. The image is very well chosen, for a certain type of inkslabs, called *ching-t'ien-yen* 井田硯, actually show the cavity for the pure water carved like a well. This line is an elaboration of a clause in the latter part of Tu Fu's 杜甫 poem 贈特進汝陽王二十韻 (Collected Works, ch. 9), where it is said: 硯寒金井水, 簷動玉壺冰.

In Chinese poetry 寒 often means " lonely." At the same time, however, this first line refers to the pond in the garden of the scholar, and thus harmonizes with the second line, which describes his library. This second line also suggests loneliness, by hinting at the story of Ch'ê Yin 車胤, a poor scholar, who had no money to buy oil for his lamp, and studied by the light of some fireflies (cf. 晉書, ch. 83). The last line refers to the ink-stone, which, when it is broken, should still be restored to its box, and also to the scholar, who, even when he dies in disgrace and poverty, should be allowed to find rest in his grave. *Kuei* is to be taken here in the meaning it has in expressions like *shih-ssû-ju-kuei* 視死如歸.

INDEX

To personal names the dates are added; other names and technical expressions are briefly explained. Items without any commentary or reference are titles of books.

E

T

V

W

Y

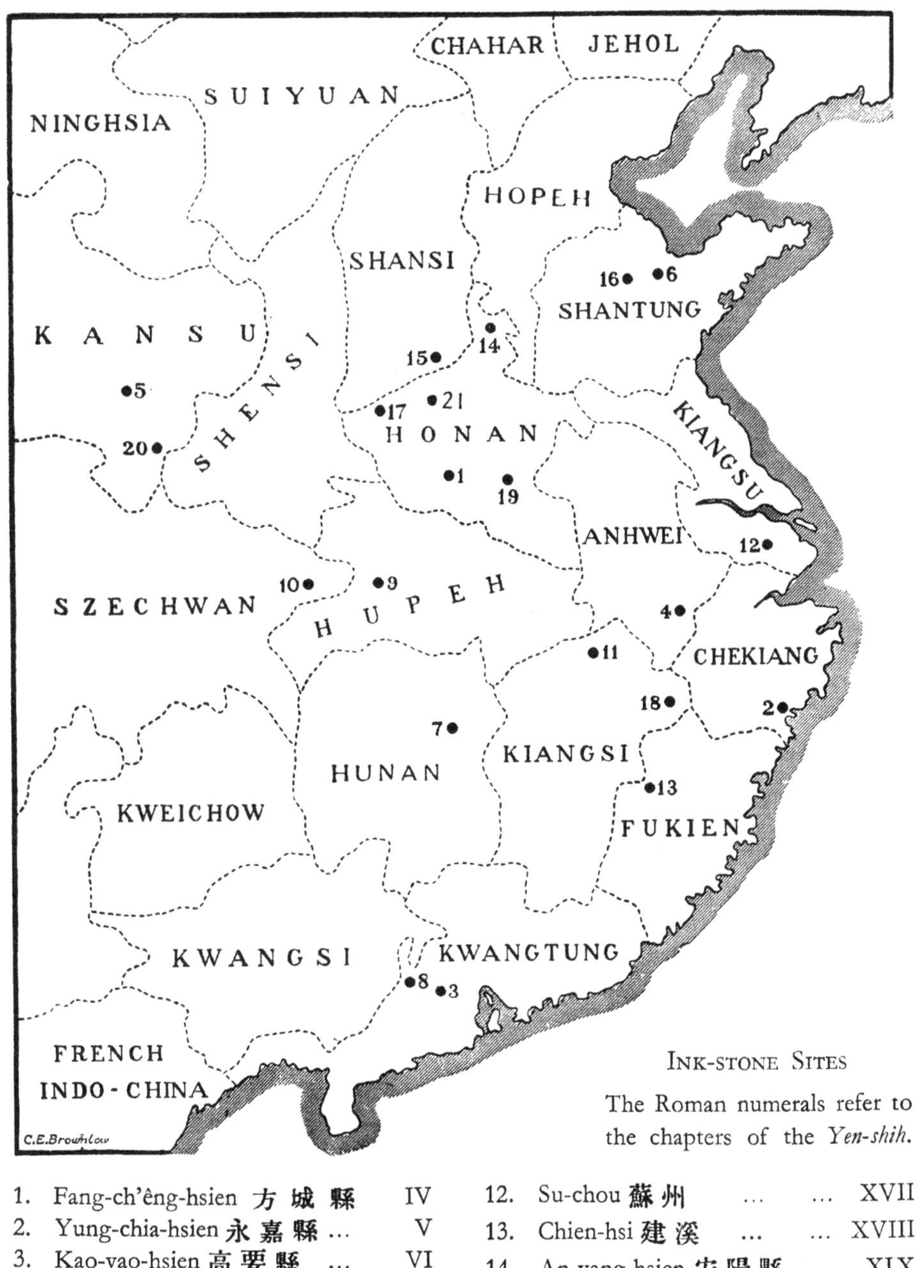

INK-STONE SITES

The Roman numerals refer to the chapters of the *Yen-shih.*

1.	Fang-ch'êng-hsien 方城縣	IV	12.	Su-chou 蘇州	XVII
2.	Yung-chia-hsien 永嘉縣 ...	V	13.	Chien-hsi 建溪	XVIII
3.	Kao-yao-hsien 高要縣 ...	VI	14.	An-yang-hsien 安陽縣 ...	XIX
4.	Hsi-hsien 歙縣	VII	15.	Chin-ch'êng-hsien 晉城縣	XX
5.	Lung-hsi-hsien 隴西縣 ...	VIII	16.	Tzŭ-ch'uan-hsien 淄川縣...	XXI
6.	I-tu 益都	X	17.	Ling-pao-hsien 靈寶縣 ...	XXIV
7.	Ch'ang-sha-hsien 長沙縣...	XII	18.	Shang-jao-hsien 上饒縣 ...	XXV
8.	Fêng-ch'uan-hsien 封川縣	XIII	19.	Ju-nan-hsien 汝南縣 ...	XXVI
9.	Tzû-kuei-hsien 秭歸縣 ...	XIV	20.	Ch'êng-hsien 成縣	XI
10.	Fêng-chieh-hsien 奉節縣...	XV	21.	Lo-yang-hsien 洛陽縣 ...	IX
11.	Chiu-chiang-hsien 九江縣	XVI			

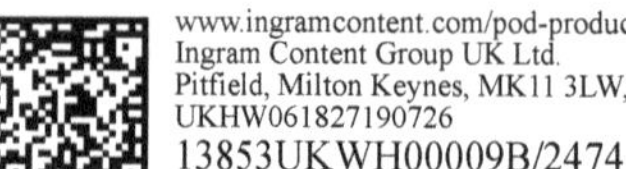

www.ingramcontent.com/pod-product-compliance
Ingram Content Group UK Ltd.
Pitfield, Milton Keynes, MK11 3LW, UK
UKHW061827190726
13853UKWH00009B/2474